MARA VORHEES

On the first day of her first visit to Kraków (on her first Lonely Planet assignment), Mara was assailed by a group of teenage boys who doused her with water. The first time, she was amused; the second time, she was angry; and the third time, she brought her own bucket. It was Lany Poniedziałek, otherwise known as 'Wet Monday'. Despite this soggy introduction, Mara fell in love with the medieval city and its millennium of history. She has since heard the *hejnał* (bugle call) hundreds of times, but she has never again had a bucket of water dumped on her head.

As a longtime student of Russia, Mara is endlessly delighted by the similarities and differences between Poland and its neighbour to the east – and she continues to torture her language teachers with her Russified Polish. She has contributed to two dozen Lonely Planet titles, most recently as the coordinating author of *Eastern Europe*.

MARA'S THANKS

Dzięki goes to the funny folks in Polish class, especially the wise and patient Ola Gołdyn and the ever-enthusiastic Jürgen Rothe; to Garrett van Reed and Martin Kitson; and most of all to Jerzy, forever my favourite travelling companion.

THE PHOTOGRAPHER

Born and raised in Warsaw, Krzysztof Dydyński discovered a passion for travelling, which took him on various trips across Europe, Asia, South America, and finally to Australia where he now lives.

Our readers Many thanks to the travellers who wrote to us with helpful hints, useful advice and interesting anecdotes. Justin Akin, Tomek Sikorski.

Cover photograph Atmospheric alfresco dining at a Cloth Hall (p45) cafe, with the Mariacka Basilica (p15) standing sentinel, Old Town; **Kevin Foy/Alamy. Internal photographs** p20 Wojtek Buss/Photolibrary; p130 EmmePi Europe/Alamy; p22 Henryk T Kaiser/Photolibrary; p21 Marka/Alamy; p18 Pegaz/Alamy; p106 Les Polders/Alamy; p19 Maurice Savage/Alamy. All other photographs by Lonely Planet Images, and by Krzysztof Dydyński except p6, p8, p15, p17, p32, p118, p120 Bruce Bi; p64 Paul Greenway; p96 Richard Nebesky; p11 Jonathan Smith; p47, p53, p79, p105 Mara Vorhees.

All images are copyright of the photographers unless otherwise indicated. Many of the images in this guide are available for licensing from **Lonely Planet Images:** lonelyplanetimages.com

Traces of memory: photography exhibition at the Galicia Jewish Museum (p70), Kazimierz

CONTENTS

Why is our travel information the best in the world? It's simple: our authors are passionate, dedicated travellers. They don't take freebies in exchange for positive coverage so you can be sure the advice you're given is impartial. They travel widely to all the popular spots, and off the beaten track. They don't research using just the internet or phone. They discover new places not included in any other guidebook. They personally visit thousands of hotels, restaurants, palaces, trails, galleries, temples and more. They speak with dozens of locals every day to make sure you get the kind of insider knowledge only a local could tell you. They take pride in getting all the details right, and in telling it how it is. Think you can do it? Find out how at **lonelyplanet.com**.

THIS IS KRAKÓW

The year is 1241. Terror has swept across Europe. It arrives on horseback, in the form of murderous marauders who destroy everything in their path, raping and pillaging as they go. The prosperous town of Kraków is not immune to the Mongol scourge.

High up in the watchtower of Mariacka Basilica, a lone fireman sees the hellions on the horizon. He sounds an alarm on his bugle, playing the haunting *hejnał* for all to hear. Before he can finish the melody, he is shot by an approaching raider. The arrow pierces his neck. The warning song is cut off mid-note, as the bugler falls to his death.

This tragic but heroic tale is the story of Kraków – a sparkling city of culture and learning, destined to endure suffering despite the valiant efforts of its citizens.

It may have been the first time in Kraków's history that this scenario was played out, but it would not be the last. Mongols, Teutonic Knights, Russians, Swedes, Austrians, Nazis and communists all brought death and destruction over the years. Yet Kraków endured.

In the 21st century, Kraków has emerged as a dynamic destination for avant-garde art, jazz music, street theatre and student life. The Old Town is a visual feast of Gothic, Renaissance and Baroque, its architecture recounting 750 years of history. The former Jewish quarters in Kazimierz and Podgórze have not forgotten their tragic past, but they too are experiencing an infusion of creative energy. For so long silent, the old synagogues now house art galleries, bookstores and cultural centres.

Up in the watchtower of Mariacka Basilica, a trumpeter still plays the haunting melody known as the *hejnał*, cutting off mid-note, as did his predecessor centuries before. Then he waves his bugle out the window; the schoolchildren cheer. We're not saying it's a true story, we're just saying it's a good story – conveying the history and heroism of the medieval city.

Top left Knights in shining armour feasting on *pierogi* (dumplings; p118) at one of Kraków's festivals (p23) **Top right** Fragments of history: commemorative wall at Remuh Cemetery (p72), Kazimierz **Bottom** Poster art bonanza: Galeria Plakatu (p52), Old Town

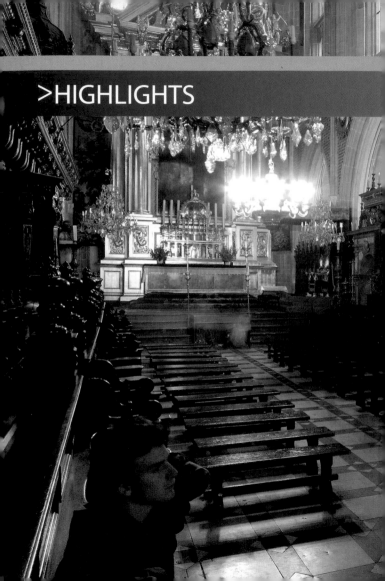

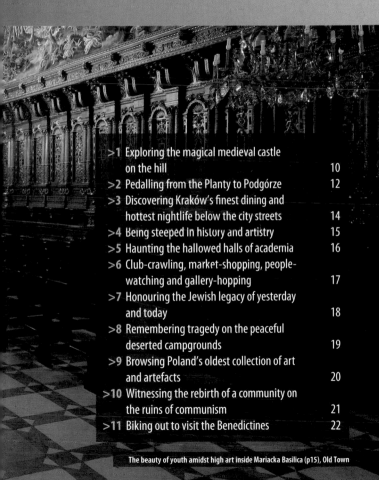

The beauty of youth amidst high art inside Mariacka Basilica (p15), Old Town

>1 WAWEL HILL

EXPLORING THE MAGICAL MEDIEVAL CASTLE ON THE HILL

Perched high atop a hill overlooking the Vistula (Wisła) River, the towers of the castle and the spires of the cathedral evoke the magic and mystery of medieval Kraków. As the residence of kings and queens for five centuries, the castle is a museum of art and history. As the burial place of the country's most esteemed heroes, the cathedral is a memorial to those who made Poland what she is today.

The first fortress was built on Wawel Hill in the 11th century but the present castle dates largely from the 16th century. Today, the grounds house a series of museums dedicated to the castle's history and the events that transpired here; see p36 for more information.

Within the castle walls, Wawel Cathedral is Poland's most significant and celebrated church. Built in 1364, this is the third church to stand on this site. It is the final resting place of Poland's most distinguished historical figures, so walking around the sarcophagi is like taking a tour through Polish history.

Among the many chapels, the showpiece is the Renaissance Sigismund Chapel, topped with a gilded half-dome. It houses the red marble tombs of King Zygmunt I and his son, Zygmunt II. The Chapel of Queen Zofia is equally impressive, with its beautiful stained glass and murals in the Art Nouveau style.

Beneath the sanctuary, there are two sets of burial chambers. The tiny Poets' Crypt contains only three tombs, including that of

STATE ROOMS

Touring all of the museums on Wawel Hill takes all day. If you only have time for one, let it be the imposing State Rooms, which have been restored to their Renaissance-era splendour and filled with antique furnishings and art. There are many architectural details to marvel at, including marble doorways, stucco ceilings and an impressive Roman Baroque fireplace. The Senate Hall walls are hung with 16th-century Flemish tapestries, the only artwork to survive from the original castle decoration. Everybody's favourite room is the Hall of Deputies, its unique coffered ceiling studded with 30 carved human heads making funny faces.

the Romantic poet Adam Mickiewicz; the dank Royal Crypts house the sarcophagi of several kings and national heroes such as Tadeusz Kościuszko and Józef Piłsudski. None of these tombs achieves the flamboyance of the Baroque silver Shrine of St Stanislaus in the centre of the cathedral. (See p72 for more on St Stanislaus.)

You can complete your cathedral tour by climbing 70 wood steps up the narrow Sigismund Tower to see the great Sigismund Bell, cast in 1520. At 2m high and weighing 11 tonnes, it's the largest historic bell in Poland.

>2 KRAKÓW BIKE TOUR

PEDALLING FROM THE PLANTY TO PODGÓRZE

Cyclists speed through the Old Town, zipping down cobblestone streets that are off-limits to cars and overtaking pedestrians without a second thought. If this looks like fun to you, you can hire two wheels for yourself and join the daily tour with Krakow Bike Tours (p147). The four-hour, 12km tour provides the perfect introduction to the city. You do not have to be an experienced rider, as the distances are not too great and most of the riding is not on the road.

The route may vary a bit, but the tour always starts at the Rynek Główny, which is still the centre of all goings-on. Then participants pedal out to the Planty (see the boxed text, p50), the green strip of parkland that circles the Old Town. The tour stops at sites along the way, including the Barbican (p46), the Collegium Maius (p16 and p46; pictured) and the Papal Window (p49).

From here, the route cuts down to the river, passing by Wawel Castle (p36) and the Dragon's Den (p38). A lovely riverside bike path leads to the Pauline Church of SS Michael & Stanislaus (p72), better known as the Skałka. A short stop allows time to take of the waters before pedalling past the Church of St Catherine (p67) and Plac Wolnica, and up to Plac Nowy. About midway through the ride, everybody is invited to rest with a snack or drink at one of the cafes on ul Szeroka (p75).

After taking a breather, the tour continues across the river in Podgórze, with stops at Plac Bohaterów Getta (p85) and Schindler's Factory (p86). Your guide will even point out places where the old ghetto wall still remains. Then enjoy a slow pedal back along the Vistula River and through the Old Town.

The tour does not allow riders to go inside the different sights, as there is not enough time. Rather, it provides an introduction, so riders can decide for themselves where they want to return for an in-depth visit. The guides are entertaining and informed, offering plenty of opinions about history, legends, food, nightlife and shopping in Kraków.

The best thing about the Kraków bike tour? Seeing the city under the power of your own two legs.

>3 KRAKÓW UNDERGROUND

DISCOVERING KRAKÓW'S FINEST DINING AND HOTTEST NIGHTLIFE BELOW THE CITY STREETS

Come in off the street. Outside the city is buzzing with the energy of the jovial crowds, but here it is quiet. The courtyard appears to be empty. But wait…there is an old stone staircase leading down into the darkness. The ceiling is low and the passage is narrow. As you descend, you feel the cool air rise to meet you. You hear voices, the clink of glasses, a few notes of music.

Rounding the corner, you emerge into a cosy cavern – a subterranean space that probably dates to the 14th century. Most buildings around Kraków have been rebuilt since that time, but they retain their original foundations. No wonder these brick walls and arcaded ceilings create an atmosphere that reeks of history and mystery.

What better place for a trendy bar or cosy cafe than a 700-year-old cellar? Visitors quickly figure out that Kraków's finest dining and hottest nightlife happens underground. For dinner, try Pod Aniołami (p57) or Aqua e Vino (p55), or drop into Black Gallery (p59) for drinks. There's dancing under the streets at Pauza (p62) or Rdza (p63). Almost all of the jazz clubs are in basement bars, including Piec'Art (p63) and Jazz Club U Muniaka (p61; pictured); hear other kinds of underground music at Jazz Rock Café (p62) or Klub Re (p62).

>4 MARIACKA BASILICA

BEING STEEPED IN HISTORY AND ARTISTRY

Rising majestically over the northeastern corner of Rynek Główny, the two uneven towers of Mariacka (St Mary's) Basilica are unmistakable landmarks. According to one bloody legend, the towers of differing heights are the result of a feud between two architect brothers who each wanted to outdo the other. This competition ended when one brother knifed the other and then killed himself out of remorse. The less dramatic truth, though, is that the 69m tower was built to hold the church bells, while the 81m tower functioned as a city watchtower. On certain days, you can climb to the top of the watchtower for fabulous views of Rynek Główny and environs.

Although there has been a church on this spot since the 1220s, the original was destroyed during the Tatar raids. The edifice you see today is a 15th-century creation.

Inside, the focal point is the magnificent Gothic altarpiece. Measuring around 13m high and 11m wide, this polychrome oak and lime pentaptych was created in the late 15th century by the Nuremburg sculptor Veit Stoss (known in Poland as Wit Stwosz). At its centre is a wonderfully expressive representation of the Assumption, while the six panels recount episodes from the life of the Virgin Mary. Other high points include the carved panels over the choir stalls and the nearby stone crucifix, also by Stoss. See p48.

>5 COLLEGIUM MAIUS

HAUNTING THE HALLOWED HALLS OF ACADEMIA

Founded in 1364, the Jagiellonian University is one of the oldest in Europe, and the Collegium Maius, dating from the 15th century, is Poland's oldest university building. The highlight is the elegant arcaded courtyard (pictured), which is free to visit. Every day at 1pm, the whimsical clock chimes the old student song 'Gaudeamus Igitur' as delicate figures troop past.

Inside, a guided tour shows visitors some of the university treasures, such as rare 16th-century astronomical instruments that were supposedly used by the university's illustrious alumnus, Nicolaus Copernicus. Check out the world's oldest existing globe, dated to 1510. Still used for ceremonial occasions, the impressive Aula is a grand hall with an original Renaissance ceiling, full of portraits of kings, professors and university benefactors.

Scientific kids will enjoy the interactive exhibition hall on the ground floor: Ancient & Modern Sciences has hands-on displays and experiments covering subjects such as alchemy. See p46.

>6 PLAC NOWY

CLUB-CRAWLING, MARKET-SHOPPING, PEOPLE-WATCHING AND GALLERY-HOPPING

For years Plac Nowy was known as Jewish Sq, thanks to the *okrąglak*, the red-brick rotunda that housed the kosher meat market. Nowadays it's more like a food court, where students and late-night noshers come to feast on *zapiekanka* (open-face sandwiches) and other cheap eats (see the boxed text, p76). Aside from attracting the hungry folk, Plac Nowy has become a beacon for artists, musicians and other bohemian types, who are attracted to the rich history and artistic appeal of the old Jewish quarter.

Cafes and clubs, such as Alchemia (p78; pictured), line this quaint city square, making it a top spot for people-watching and club-crawling (see p77). The surrounding streets contain an ever-growing number of art galleries, while a flea and farmers market (p74) takes place on the square itself. So even though this square dates back to the founding of Kazimierz in 1335, it deserves its title as Plac Nowy, or 'New Sq', for its ever-adapting currency and creativity.

>7 JEWISH CULTURE FESTIVAL
HONOURING THE JEWISH LEGACY OF YESTERDAY AND TODAY

It may be true that present-day Kraków is home to only about 200 Jews, but Jewish culture is thriving in this city, thanks to the annual festival that takes place in Kazimierz (see p25). The festival opens on a Friday night with a traditional ceremony of Kabbalat Shabbat, or 'welcoming the sabbath'. The next 10 days are packed with Jewish ceremonies, theatre, film, music, art exhibitions, tours and workshops in venues all around Kazimierz.

Pre-eminent Jewish scholars share their knowledge of language, music, dance, art and cooking, with several workshops designed specifically for kids. The grand finale is a huge open-air concert of contemporary Jewish music, which draws crowds of up to 15,000 to ul Szeroka. See also p79.

>8 PŁASZÓW CAMP

REMEMBERING TRAGEDY ON THE PEACEFUL DESERTED CAMPGROUNDS

Starting in October 1942, Jews were deported from the Kraków ghetto to the Płaszów concentration camp in the southern outskirts of town. Six months later, the ghetto was liquidated and all of its residents were sent to the now-notorious camp. Over the course of the next two years, thousands would die from disease, starvation and mass executions. In early 1945, the remaining prisoners commenced a death march to Auschwitz, where they would be killed on arrival. The Nazis destroyed the camp as they retreated, so there was nothing left for the Soviet troops to liberate when they arrived on 20 January 1945.

Today, the deserted campgrounds are a strangely peaceful place, belying the tragedy of a previous century. The only constructions are a few monuments scattered around the grounds. Walking trails crisscross the overgrown fields. Nature has been allowed to take over, either to block the memory or to abet the healing, or both. See the boxed text, p88, for details.

HIGHLIGHTS

>9 PRINCES CZARTORYSKI MUSEUM

BROWSING POLAND'S OLDEST COLLECTION OF ART AND ARTEFACTS

It was in 1796 that Princess Izabela Czartoryska established the first historical museum in Poland, in the town of Puławy. The collection was brought to Kraków in 1874 and housed in the old Arsenal in the city walls. This former private collection now represents one of the city's richest museums (see p50).

Among the first exhibits to greet visitors are an assemblage of Turkish weaponry, armour, saddles and rugs and a campaign tent recovered after the 1683 Battle of Vienna. The archaeology gallery contains some of the museum's most fascinating treasures, including ancient Egyptian mummies, Etruscan sarcophagi, Babylonian cylinder seals, Greek vases and Roman statues. Other oddities on this floor include the death mask of Frédéric Chopin and a tricorn hat that belonged to the last king of Poland, Stanisław August Poniatowski.

It's the art gallery upstairs, though, that's the main draw. Here you'll find many masterpieces by European artists, including the stunning *Lady with an Ermine* (c 1482) by Leonardo da Vinci, and the *Landscape with the Good Samaritan* (1638) by Rembrandt. There's no arguing against the fact that the Czartoryski princes had good taste.

>10 NOWA HUTA

WITNESSING THE REBIRTH OF A COMMUNITY ON THE RUINS OF COMMUNISM

Although Nowa Huta is only 12km east of the Old Town, it feels like it's much further east. Tram 4 takes you from medieval Poland to communist Poland in about 20 minutes.

The 'New Steelworks' was built in 1949 as an idealistic social experiment. It was not only a factory, but also a planned city, carefully laid out according to utopian principles. This plan is still evident in its wide avenues and green gardens. The architecture is an incongruous mix: Renaissance, which was supposed to be Poland's 'national form'; socialist realist, which was the preferred style of communism; and postmodern, which was added during the 1970s and 1980s.

By most counts, the socialist experiment failed. Indeed, the steelworkers of Nowa Huta were active in Solidarity, which was a key player in bringing down the communist regime.

Nonetheless, Nowa Huta has always been a progressive place. Even today, the neighbourhood is home to the city's most adventurous theatre (p106), film (see the boxed text, p25) and music (p25) events. Yet it still retains its precapitalist sheen (or lack of sheen, perhaps). And that's what makes this place so intriguing; it's as if it's balancing precariously between the past and the future, but the present is nowhere to be found. See the boxed text, p106.

HIGHLIGHTS

>11 TYNIEC

BIKING OUT TO VISIT THE BENEDICTINES

A paved bike path follows the south bank of the Vistula River from the centre of Kraków all the way out to the Benedictine abbey (pictured; see the boxed text, p98) at Tyniec, about 12km west. This is part of the Amber Trail, a hiking and biking trail that runs from Budapest to Kraków (and eventually on to the Baltic Coast). The scenic byway offers wonderful views of the Vistula River, Wawel Castle (p36) and Silver Mountain (p94), before it finally turns inland to the monastery.

The church and surrounding grounds are perched in a stunning position overlooking the river. The Benedictines have occupied this spot for almost 1000 years – since the founding of the monastery in 1044. The current Baroque church dates to the 17th century, though you can see evidence of its earlier origins. West of the church, inside the building, the original stone foundations are uncovered and protected behind glass.

The abbey is small, but the Benedictines are welcoming, offering daily Mass and occasional concerts in their beautiful church. There is also a small store selling Benedictine products, including honey, jam, cheese and other goodies made by holy men. That's got to be good for you.

>KRAKÓW DIARY

When the weather starts to warm up, so do the celebrations. Kraków may seem quiet during the winter months, but when spring arrives, locals take to the streets, squares and cellars. Starting in May, the Rynek Główny is a nonstop venue for music and more. To get the low-down, visit Kraków Info (www.krakow-info.com) or Cracow Life (www.cracow-life.com).

Street performers hit the Rynek Główny (p40) for some spring shenanigans

JANUARY & FEBRUARY

Shanties International Festival of Sailors' Songs

Międzynarodowy Festiwal Piosenki Żeglarskiej Shanties; www.shanties.pl

You might think Kraków is a city of landlubbers due to its inland locale, but this competition at the end of February has attracted singing sailors for 25 years.

Dancers swirling in traditional dress create a chain of joy at Juvenalia

MARCH & APRIL

Misteria Paschalia

www.misteriapaschalia.pl

During the week before Easter, Kraków is filled with holy songs as it hosts the world's best-known performers of sacral music.

Culture for Tolerance Festival

Kultura dla Tolerancji; www.tolerancja.org.pl

Polish Pride. This controversial GLBT event is a weekend of movies, art exhibits and queer cafe talks, as well as the divisive March for Tolerance. (Poland is much more Catholic, and conservative, than other European countries; see p144.) Held in April.

MAY

Juvenalia

Juwenalia; www.juwenalia.krakow.pl

Students celebrate in the streets for four days, with dancing, singing and fancy dress.

Cracovia Marathon

www.cracoviamaraton.pl

Run from the Old Town, around the Błonia Park, out to Nowa Huta and back.

Krakow International Film Festival

Krakowski Festiwal Filmowy; www.krakowfilmfestival.pl

A long-running festival that shows hundreds of international films at various venues.

JUNE

Dragon's Parade
Parada Smaków; www.paradasmokow.pl
Two days of puppetry, music and theatre celebrating the Wawel Dragon. The parade runs from Wawel Castle to the Rynek Główny.

Lajkonik Pageant
www.mhk.pl
A comical, Cracovian figure disguised as a Tatar riding a wooden horse, Lajkonik parades from Zwierzyniec to the Rynek Główny.

JULY

Jewish Culture Festival
Festiwal Kultury Żydowskiej;
www.jewishfestival.pl
The biggest Jewish festival in Europe takes place in Kazimierz during the first week in July. See also p18.

International Festival of Street Theatre
Międzynarodowy Festiwal Teatrów Ulicznych; www.teatrkto.pl
Body language and other nonverbal communication make the drama on the Rynek Główny enjoyable for all audiences.

Crossroads
Rozstaje; www.rozstaje.pl
This long-running festival of traditional music features bands from all over Central and Eastern Europe.

IN THE NEIGHBOURHOOD
Not all of the action goes down on the Rynek Główny. The city's neighbourhoods host festivities that highlight their diversity and vibrancy.
Rękawka (www.podgorze.pl; Podgórze) A spring festival dating to pagan times. Festivities take place near the Church of St Benedict (p84) on the Tuesday after Easter.
International Soup Festival (Międzynarodowy Festiwal Zupy; www.teatrkto.pl; Kazimierz) A day in May dedicated to cooking and eating soup on Plac Nowy.
Nowa Huta Film Festival (Nowohutcki Festiwal Filmowy; www.nhfestiwal.pl; Nowa Huta) Happens in August.

AUGUST & SEPTEMBER

Music in Old Kraków
Muzyka w Starem Krakowie;
www.capellacracoviensls.pl
During the last two weeks of August, the Capella Cracoviensis chamber orchestra and vocal ensemble performs with guest artists in churches, museums and historic halls.

Sacrum-Profanum Festival
www.sacrumprofanum.pl
This unique event in September celebrates contemporary 'classical' music. Takes place in the halls of the steelworks and other venues around Nowa Huta.

Red roses and ribbons celebrate gay pride

OCTOBER & NOVEMBER

Unsound Festival

http://unsound.pl

A week of electronica in October, featuring films, performance art and interactive exhibits.

All Saints & All Souls Days

Cemeteries light up on 1 and 2 November, the Catholic holidays to honour the dead.

Festival of Polish Music

Festiwal Muzyki Polskiej; www.fmp.org.pl

A week in November packed with concerts by Polish composers at Kraków theatres.

DECEMBER

Christmas Market & Christmas Cribs

www.mhk.pl

During December, the Rynek Główny takes on a particular magic, as it's covered with snow and decorated for the holidays. Vendors sell souvenirs and mulled wine to warm the winter shoppers. Local artists construct elaborate Nativity scenes, which are displayed near the statue of Adam Mickiewicz.

New Year's Eve

Ring in the New Year on Rynek Główny, with free concerts and fun. At midnight, bells sound from the Mariacka Basilica and fireworks light the sky.

Sombre exhibit at the Pharmacy Under the Eagle museum (p85), Podgórze

ITINERARIES

DAY ONE

On your first day in Kraków get an early start to beat the crowds to Wawel Hill (p36). After exploring the magnificent castle and cathedral, take a break for lunch at La Campana Trattoria (p57). Stop to admire the artistry in the Basilica of St Francis (p44) and to catch a glimpse of John Paul II waving from the Papal Window (p49). From here, continue on into the heart of the Old Town to the bustling Rynek Główny. To get the big picture, climb the Town Hall Tower (p50). Otherwise, stroll through the Cloth Hall (p45) and listen to the *hejnał* (bugle call) from the Mariacka Basilica (p48). Enjoy dinner in the cellar at Chimera Restaurant (p56), then get into the jazz at Piec'Art (p63) or Jazz Club U Muniaka (p61).

DAY TWO

Spend your morning in Kazimierz, starting with a delicious breakfast at Bagel Mama (p75), followed by a few hours at the excellent and moving Galicia Jewish Museum (p70). Stroll down ul Szeroka, stopping to pay your respects at the Remuh Synagogue & Cemetery (p72) or to peruse the collection at the Old Synagogue (p71). For lunch, sample one of a zillion kinds of *pierogi* (dumplings) at Pierożki U Vincenta (p76). In the afternoon, wander across the river into Podgórze to Plac Bohaterów Getta (p85), the centre of the former Jewish ghetto. Pop into the museum at the Pharmacy Under the Eagle (p85) or alternatively at Schindler's Factory (p86). In the evening, head back to Plac Nowy for dinner at Kuchnia i Wino (p75), drinks at Mleczarnia (p78) or music at Alchemia (p78).

DAY THREE

Catch the train to Oświęcim to visit the Auschwitz-Birkenau State Museum (p111). If you wish to visit both sites – and you do – this is an all-day affair with 90 minutes of travel time in each direction.

Alternatively, Wieliczka Salt Mine (p113) and Nowa Huta (see the boxed text, p106) also offer unique excursions that are less of an expedition.

Top Impressive sculpture hand-carved entirely from salt, Chapel of the Blessed Kinga, Wieliczka Salt Mine (p113)
Bottom Ornate detailing in the still-functioning Remuh Synagogue (p72), Kazimierz

RAINY DAY

You could probably spend all day at the enormous National Museum (p94), with its vastly varied collections. But we'll just give you the morning – plenty of time to investigate the intriguing Gallery of 20th-Century Polish Painting. Make your way to Dynia (p97) for lunch, then spend the afternoon browsing for books at Massolit Books & Café (p95). If you find something good to read, you might just hunker down at Café Szafe (p97) and wait out the weather.

SUNNY DAY

The sun has come out and you want to go out and play. Consider spending the day in Podgórze – investigate the mysterious Church of St Benedict (p84) and climb up to Krakus Mound (p84) for fabulous views all around. Continue on to the peaceful and mournful grounds of the former Płaszów camp (see the boxed text, p88). Alternatively, catch the bus out to forested Las Wolski, where you can visit the animals at the Zoological Gardens (p95) and climb to the sky on Piłsudski Mound (p95). You can also hike through the forest to the walled Monastery of Camaldolese Monks (p94), but most of the time only men are allowed to enter.

MONDAY

Many museums are closed on Monday, so you may feel you have been stranded with nothing to do. Hardly! Keep in mind that all churches and synagogues are open on Monday, as are outdoor attractions such

FORWARD PLANNING

One month before you go Start walking. Kraków is a walking city, so make sure your feet are ready for it. Log onto the Kraków Post (www.krakowpost.com) to see what's new with politics, food, fashion and culture. Scan the City Life section to find out what's going down when you'll be in town.

One week before you go Buy tickets for the Opera Krakowska (p104) or the Filharmonia Krakowska (p98). Make a dinner reservation at Chimera Restaurant (p56) or Miód Malina (p57). Reserve your time for a tour of the Collegium Maius (p46) and the Royal Private Apartments (p39) at Wawel Castle.

One day before you go Visit Cracow-Life (www.cracow-life.com) to see the weather forecast. No matter what it says, be sure to pack a sweater.

as Kościuszko Mound (p91) and the Defensive Walls (p46). On Wawel Hill, the Crown Treasury & Armoury (p38) and Lost Wawel (p38) are not only open on Monday (until 1pm), they are free of charge on Monday between April and October. A few museums are open for half a day, so if you get up early enough you can visit the Archaeological Museum (p44), Collegium Maius (p46) or the Old Synagogue (p71). The Galicia Jewish Museum (p70) may be the only museum that stays open all day on Monday.

A peaceful autumn stroll through Las Wolski (p95), western Kraków

>NEIGHBOURHOODS

A candlelit beer (with onlookers) at cosy Alchemia (p78), Kazimierz

NEIGHBOURHOODS

If the map of Kraków is a dartboard, most travellers aim for the bullseye. That would be the Rynek Główny – the enormous medieval market square that has been the focal point of cultural and commercial activity for centuries.

If travellers don't hit the Rynek dead on, they usually come pretty close, spending most of their time on the cobblestone streets that sprout out from the square and form the Old Town.

As you might guess, the Old Town is the most ancient and most evocative part of Kraków. Indeed, in its earliest days, this was the city. The green leafy strip that circles the centre (the Planty) marks the location of the former city walls. At the southern end, the medieval fortress tops Wawel Hill. This is what travellers come to see.

The bullseye is not the only way to score, however. Kraków's richness stems from its diversity and complexity, which becomes apparent only when you leave the Old Town. In the southeast, Kazimierz is the former Jewish district, now a bohemian outpost. Further south, on the Vistula (Wisła) River, Podgórze is an important though tragic historic site – the location of the Jewish ghetto and of a Nazi concentration camp during WWII.

Heading east, most travellers will not venture further than the main train station. Just a little further, however, you'll come across the brand-new Opera Krakowska, a startling but stunning example of contemporary Polish architecture. And in the far eastern suburbs, Nowa Huta is an intriguing relic of communist Kraków.

West of the centre, Zwierzyniec offers an eclectic array of attractions, from the masterpieces at the National Museum to the vista from Kościuszko Mound. Those who seek an escape from the urban atmosphere can retreat to Las Wolski or follow the Vistula River all the way to the Benedictine abbey at Tyniec.

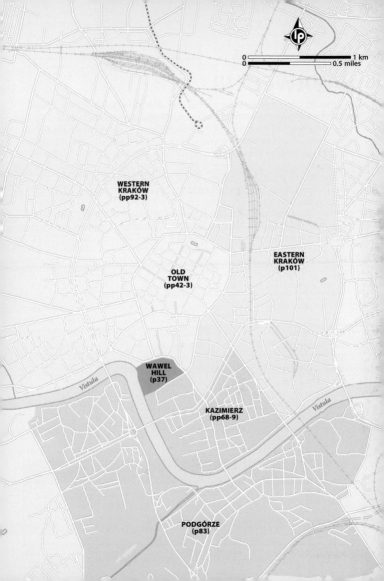

0 | 1 km
0 | 0.5 miles

WESTERN
KRAKÓW
(pp92-3)

EASTERN
KRAKÓW
(p101)

OLD
TOWN
(pp42-3)

WAWEL
HILL
(p37)

Vistula

KAZIMIERZ
(pp68-9)

Vistula

PODGÓRZE
(p83)

>WAWEL HILL

The symbol of a nation, Wawel Hill is the silent guardian of a millennium of Polish history. The hilltop castle was the seat of kings for over 500 years, from the earliest days of the Polish state. The mighty cathedral was the final resting place for many of them. For much of Polish history, Wawel was the site of the most solemn ceremonies and most celebrated moments.

The way to Wawel Hill begins at the southern end of ul Kanonicza, from where a lane leads uphill, past the equestrian statue of Tadeusz Kościuszko, and into a vast open central square. Buy tickets to the exhibits (minus the cathedral) in the **visitors centre** (☎ 012 422 5155; www.wawel .krakow.pl; 🕑 9am-6pm) in the southwestern part of the complex. Alternatively, you can prebook your tickets at the **Tourist Service Office** (☎ 012 422 1697; Bldg 9, Wawel 5; 🕑 9am-4pm Mon-Fri, 10am-5pm Sat & Sun).

WAWEL HILL

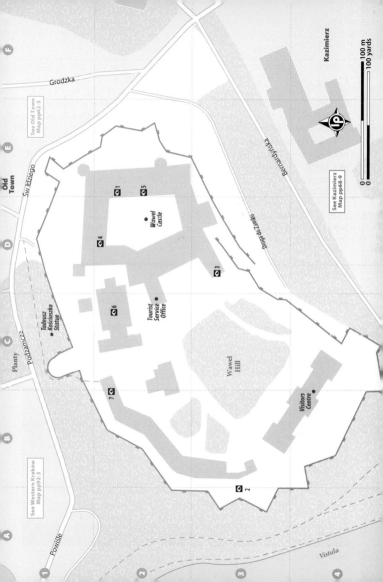

See Western Kraków
Map pp92-3

Powiśle

Planty

Podzamcze

Św. Idziego

Old
Town

Grodzka

See Old Town
Map pp42-3

Kazimierz

See Kazimierz
Map pp68-9

Bernardyńska

Droga do Zamku

Vistula

Tadeusz
Kościuszko
Statue

Tourist
Service
Office

Wawel
Castle

Wawel
Hill

Visitors
Centre

1
5
4
3
6
7
2

100 m
100 yards

👁 SEE

🔲 CROWN TREASURY & ARMOURY

Skarbiec Korony i Zbrojownia; adult/concession 17/10zł, Mon Apr-Oct free, Sun Nov-Mar free; 🕑 **9.30am-1pm Mon, to 5pm Tue-Fri, 11am-6pm Sat & Sun**

The treasury's prize possession is the Szczerbiec, or 'Jagged Sword', used at Polish coronations since 1320. Otherwise, most of the good stuff was plundered and pillaged by various occupying armies. The adjacent armoury features an enormous collection of weapons from crossbows to cannons.

🔲 DRAGON'S DEN

Smocza Jama; admission 3zł; 🕑 **10am-6pm Jul & Aug, to 5pm Apr, May, Sep & Oct**

Complete your Wawel Hill tour by visiting the dragon's lair, one-time home to the legendary fire-breather. Descend 135 steps through the damp cave, emerging on the Vistula (Wisła) River's bank. The bronze likeness is by contemporary sculptor Bronisław Chromy.

🔲 LOST WAWEL

Wawel Zaginiony; adult/concession 8/5zł, Mon Apr-Oct free, Sun Nov-Mar free; 🕑 **9.30am-1pm Mon, to 5pm Tue-Fri, 11am-6pm Sat & Sun**

This archaeological exhibit traces the history of Wawel Castle, starting with the ruins of the 10th-century Rotunda of SS Felix and Adauctus. Remnants from other eras include the 16th-century stables and the Renaissance kitchens.

🔲 ORIENTAL ART EXHIBIT

Wystawa Sztuka Wschodu; adult/concession 7/4zł, Sun Nov-Mar free; 🕑 **9.30am-5pm Tue-Fri, 11am-6pm Sat & Sun**

Celebrating Poland's proudest moment, this exhibit shows off the loot from the Battle of Vienna. The

---

SMOK THE MAGIC DRAGON

Long ago, during Prince Krak's reign, a nasty dragon lived in the cave below Wawel Hill, terrorising Kraków town. A fire-breathing menace, the scaly *smok* ravaged residents and livestock, leaving death and destruction in his wake. His favourite food was beautiful young virgins.

Prince Krak feared for the life of his own daughter Wanda, and he offered her hand in marriage to any suitor who could slay the dragon. Many died trying.

Finally, a poor young cobbler came up with a scheme to trick the dragon. He stuffed a sheep with sulphur and left the tasty morsel outside the dragon's lair. The dragon fell for it. He devoured the sheep, then retreated to the Vistula River to quench his unbearable thirst. He drained the river, causing his stomach to swell and inciting a massive explosion.

The dragon was defeated! The cobbler was a hero! The virgins were safe! And Wanda and the cobbler lived happily ever after.

Catholic Poland's pride and joy: Wawel Cathedral

collection of 17th-century Turkish banners and weaponry is displayed along with a variety of Persian carpets, Chinese and Japanese ceramics, and other Asian antiques.

◙ ROYAL PRIVATE APARTMENTS
Prywatne Apartamenty Królewskie; adult/concession 24/18zł, Sun Nov-Mar free; ☽ **9.30am-5pm Tue-Fri, 11am-6pm Sat & Sun**
This guided tour leads you through the castle's sumptuously decorated private quarters, giving an inkling of how the Polish royal family lived. The rooms are adorned with an impressive collection of French and Flemish tapestries.

◙ STATE ROOMS
Komnaty Królewskie; adult/concession 17/10zł, Sun Nov-Mar free; ☽ **9.30am-5pm Tue-Fri, 11am-6pm Sat & Sun**
The castle's official State Rooms, or Royal Chambers, have been restored to their original Renaissance and Baroque styles. The two-dozen 2nd-floor rooms are crammed with period paintings, tapestries and works of art. The highlight is the **Hall of Deputies**: its fantastic coffered ceiling is studded with 30 individually carved and painted wooden heads staring back at you. See also p10.

◙ WAWEL CATHEDRAL & MUSEUM
Katedra Wawelska; ☎ **012 422 2643; Wawel 3; adult/concession 10/5zł, audio tour 5zł;** ☽ **9am-4pm or 5.15pm Mon-Sat, 12.15-4pm or 5.15pm Sun**
Poland's most important church is the 1364 Gothic beauty that sits atop Wawel Hill. Admire the central silver Shrine of St Stanislaus and the many chapels that ring the sanctuary, before descending into the tiny **Poets' Crypt** and the mazelike **Royal Crypts**. Finally, you can climb the 70 wooden steps to the top of the **Sigismund Tower** to see the great Sigismund Bell. See also p10.

Opposite the cathedral is the Cathedral Museum, which displays various ecclesiastical treasures and royal funerary regalia.

>OLD TOWN

Certainly Kraków must have seemed the centre of the universe in medieval times. Back then, the city consisted solely of the Stare Miasto, or Old Town, surrounded by formidable defensive walls. It centred on the majestic market square, the Rynek Główny, which was the largest city square in Europe, measuring an even 200m by 200m. Majestic buildings dotted the square, including the Town Hall and the Cloth Hall, both of which still exist in various forms. Then, as now, the surrounding streets were neatly laid out in their grid pattern and crammed with Gothic churches and noble palaces. There are only a few remnants of the defensive walls, but the Old Town is still encircled by the Planty, a narrow parkland that was once the moat.

Much remains from Kraków's earliest days, from the arcaded cellars on the Rynek Główny to the haunting melody that rings out from the Mariacka steeple. Contemporary Kraków is a dynamic and developing city, but the Old Town has been purposefully and perpetually suspended in time.

This time-travel effect is only slightly marred by the hordes of school children, stag parties and tour groups frolicking around the ancient streets. (It may be the largest medieval square in Europe, but the Rynek Główny still feels crowded at the peak of the summer tourist season.) The clip-clop of horses competes with the whir of electric golf carts, and tour guides vie for attention with folk singers and human statues; a festive though frenetic atmosphere pervades the Old Town, especially along the Royal Way (ul Floriańska, Rynek Główny and ul Grodzka).

Fortunately, it's easy to retreat to a quiet side street, a tranquil church, or a hidden courtyard…where the magic and mystery of the Middle Ages endures.

OLD TOWN

🅒 SEE
Archaeological
  Museum **1** C6
Archdiocesan Museum ..**2** C7
Barbican **3** E1
Basilica of St Francis **4** C5
Bishop Erazm Ciołek
  Palace **5** C7
Church of SS Peter
  & Paul **6** D7
Church of St Adalbert **7** C4
Church of St Andrew **8** D7
Cloth Hall **9** C4
Collegium Maius **10** B4
Cricoteka Archive **11** C6
Defensive Walls .....(see 13)
Defensive Walls ....(see 3)
Dominican Church of
  the Holy Trinity **12** D5
Florian Gate **13** E2
Franciscan
  Monastery **14** C5
Gallery of 19th-Century
  Polish Painting ....(see 9)
Hipolit House **15** D4
Kantor's Atelier **16** B4
Krzysztofory Palace **17** C3
Mariacka Basilica **18** D4
Matejko House **19** E2
Palace of Fine Arts **20** B2
Papal Window **21** B5
Pharmacy Museum **22** D3
Princes Czartoryski
  Museum **23** D2
Town Hall Tower **24** C4
Wyspiański Museum **25** C3

🅢 SHOP
Alhena **26** D4
Andrzej Mleczko
  Gallery **27** D3
Boruni Gallery **28** C7
EMPiK **29** D4
Galeria AG **30** D5
Galeria Bukowski **31** D4
Galeria Plakatu **32** D5
Galeria Skarbiec **33** C6
Jan Fejkiel Gallery **34** C7
Krakowski Kredens **35** C5
Labirynt **36** E2
Mikołajczyki
  Amber **37** C7
My Gallery **38** B5
Punkt **39** C2
Salon Antyków
  Pasja **40** B3
Szambelan **41** C5
Toruńskie Pierniki **42** C5
Wedel Pijalnia
  Czekolady **43** D3

🍴 EAT
Aqua e Vino **44** B4
Bar Grodzki **45** C6
Bar Smaczny **46** E3
Casa della Pizza **47** D4
Chimera Restaurant **48** B4
Chimera Salad Bar .....(see 48)
Cyrano de Bergerac **49** D2
Farina **50** D2
Farinella Kuchnia
  & Bar **51** B4
Green Way **52** E4
La Campana
  Trattoria **53** C7
Miód Malina **54** C6
Orient Ekspres **55** D5
Pod Aniołami **56** C6
Pod Krzyżykiem **57** C3
Polskie Smaki **58** C2
Szambelan ....(see 41)
Wentzl **59** C4

🅨 DRINK
Black Gallery **60** E4
Café Bunkier **61** B3
Café Camelot **62** D3
Café Philo **63** E4
Cieplarnia **64** C5
Jama Michalika **65** E2
Nowa Prowincja **66** C5
Tram Bar **67** D5
Vinoteka La
  Bodega **68** C2

⭐ PLAY
Bonerowski Palace **69** C3
Church of SS Peter
  & Paul ....(see 6)
Church of St Giles **70** C8
Cień Klub **71** D2
Frantic **72** B3
Harris Piano Jazz
  Bar **73** B4
Jazz Club U
  Muniaka **74** D3
Jazz Rock Café ....(see 68)
Klub Re **75** E4
Lizard King **76** C3
Pauza **77** D3
Piec' Art **78** B3
Piwnica Pod
  Baranami **79** B4
Polonia House **80** C5
Rdza ....(see 66)
Stalowe Magnolie **81** D2
Stary Teatr **82** B3
Teatr im J
  Słowackiego **83** E2

Please see over for map

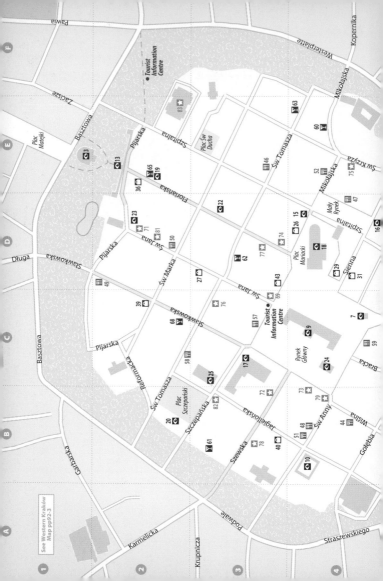

See Western Kraków Map pp2–3

Pawia

Kopernika

Westerplatte

Zacisze

Basztowa

• Tourist Information Centre

Plac Matejki

Pijarska

Szpitalna

83 ★

Plac Św Ducha

Sw Tomasza

63

60

Mikołajska

Św Krzyża

3

13

65 ▼ 19

36

Floriańska

22

46

52

47

Mały Rynek

Szpitalna

75

Długa

Sławkowska

Pijarska

23 71

81

50 ▼

Św Jana

26 15

74

18

16

27

62 ▼

77 ★

Plac Mariacki

29

Sienna 31

49

Św Marka

43

69

Św Jana

76

Basztowa

Pijarska

39

68 ▼

Sławkowska

57 ▼

Tourist Information Centre

9

7

24

Bracka

59

Garbarska

Reformacka

58

Św Tomasza

25

17

72 ★

Rynek Główny

73 ★

79 ★

Plac Szczepański

82 ★

Szczepańska

Jagiellońska

20

61 ▼

Szewska

78

40

51 48

Św Anny

44

Gołębia

Wiślna

10

Podwale

Karmelicka

Krupnicza

Straszewskiego

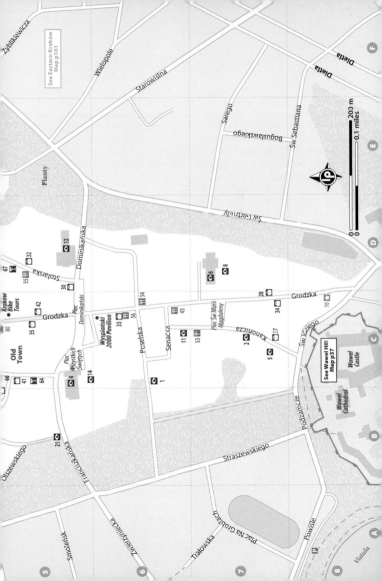

See Eastern Krakow Map p101

Zyblikiewicza

Wielopole

Starowiślna

Sarego

Bogusławskiego

Św Sebastiana

Dietla

Dietla

Planty

Św Gertrudy

0   200 m
0   0.1 miles

Dominikańska

Stolarska

12

67
55
32

30

Kraków
Bike Tours
80

Grodzka

35 42

Plac
Dominikański

54

33

Poselska

56

11 45

Plac Św Marii
Magdaleny

28

34

Grodzka

70

6

8

53

2

5

Kanonicza

37

Św Idziego

See Wawel Hill
Map p37

Wawel
Castle

Wawel
Cathedral

Podzamcze

Wyspiański
2000 Pavilion

Senacka

Plac
Wszystkich
Świętych

4

14

1

Old
Town

66
41 64
21

Straszewskiego

Otszewskiego

Franciszkańska

Zwierzyniecka

Smoleńsk

Plac Na Groblach

Tralowska

Powiśle

Vistula

👁 SEE

👁 ARCHAEOLOGICAL MUSEUM

Muzeum Archeologiczne; ☎ 012 422 7100; www.ma.krakow.pl, in Polish; ul Poselska 3; adult/concession 7/5zł, Sun free; 🕙 9am-2pm Mon-Wed, 2-6pm Thu, 10am-2pm Fri & Sun; 🚊 6, 8, 10, 18
In case you were wondering what went on in Małopolska before the founding of Kraków, this museum presents the region's history from the Palaeolithic period up until the early Middle Ages. The lovely gardens are laid out with rose bushes, magnolia trees and contemporary sculpture.

👁 ARCHDIOCESAN MUSEUM

Muzeum Archidiecezjalne; ☎ 012 421 8963; www.muzeumkra.diecezja.pl; ul

---

WORTH THE TRIP: NIEPOŁOMICE
Due to ongoing renovations at the **Cloth Hall** (opposite), the Gallery of 19th-Century Polish Painting had temporarily relocated to the **Royal Castle at Niepołomice** (☎ 012 261 9851; www .muzeum.niepolomice.pl; ul Zamkowa 2, Niepołomice; adult/concession 8/6zł; 🕙 10am-5pm), 25km east of Kraków. There is only one direct bus to Niepołomice (departing from the main bus station), so you will likely have to make a connection in Wieliczka. The gallery is expected to return to the Cloth Hall in 2010.

Kanonicza 21; adult/concession 5/3zł; 🕙 10am-4pm Tue-Fri, to 3pm Sat & Sun; 🚊 6, 8, 10, 18
This 14th-century town house holds a collection of religious sculpture and painting, dating from the 13th to the 16th centuries. Most visitors come to see where Karol Wojtyła (the late Pope John Paul II) lived from 1952 to 1967. The exhibit includes plenty of personal paraphernalia, such as the papal skis, as well as a treasury of gifts that he received.

👁 BASILICA OF ST FRANCIS

Bazylika Św Franciszka; Plac Wszystkich Świętych 5; 🚊 6, 8, 18
Duck into the dark basilica on a sunny day to admire the artistry of Stanisław Wyspiański, who designed the fantastic Art Nouveau stained-glass windows. The multicoloured deity in the chancel above the organ loft is a masterpiece. From the transept, you can also enter the Gothic cloister of the **Franciscan Monastery** to admire the fragments of 15th-century frescos.

👁 BISHOP ERAZM CIOŁEK PALACE

☎ 012 424 9370; www.muzeum.krakow .pl; ul Kanonicza 17; adult/concession 10/5zł, Sun free; 🕙 10am-6pm Tue-Sat, to 4pm Sun; 🚊 6, 8, 10, 18; ♿
Quaint, cobblestoned Kanonicza is the perfect street to put a palace

and fill it with age-old paintings and sculpture. This newish branch of the National Museum contains two exhibits of religious artwork. The Art of Old Poland (12th to 18th centuries) includes loads of Gothic paintings, altar pieces and an entire room devoted to Veit Stoss. The second exhibit focuses on Orthodox art, which means iconography, from the eastern regions.

CHURCH OF SS PETER & PAUL

Kościół Św Piotra i Pawła; ul Grodzka 54; 6, 8, 10, 18

The first Baroque building in Kraków, the Church of SS Peter & Paul was erected by the Jesuits.

Designed on the Latin cross layout and topped with a large skylit dome, the church has a refreshingly sober interior. The elaborate facade contrasts dramatically with the austere Romanesque exterior of the **Church of St Andrew** next door.

CLOTH HALL

Sukiennice; Rynek Główny 1; 1, 2, 3, 7, 8, 13, 15

Bedecked with gargoyles, the Renaissance centrepiece of the Rynek Główny was once the centre of Kraków's rag trade. The ground floor now holds a tatty tourist market, while the 1st floor is the location of the **Gallery of 19th-Century Polish Painting** (Galeria Sztuki Polskiej

Souvenir-searching fervour at the Cloth Hall's tourist market

XX Wieku). The four-room gallery represents the best of Polish portraiture, landscapes and historical painting, the highlight being Jan Matejko's *The Prussian Homage*.

⬤ COLLEGIUM MAIUS

☎ 012 422 0549; www.maius.uj.edu.pl; ul Jagiellońska 15; adult/concession 12/6zł, after 2pm Tue free; ☷ 10am-3pm Mon, Wed & Fri, to 6pm Tue & Thu, to 2pm Sat Apr-Oct, 10am-3pm Mon-Fri, to 2pm Sat Nov-Mar; ☒ 2, 3, 6, 8, 18; ♿

The oldest surviving university building in Poland is the Collegium Maius, the Gothic structure that was built as part of the Kraków Academy. Guided tours (1pm, in English) give a glimpse at the historic interiors, as well as fascinating old scientific artefacts.

In summer it's advisable to reserve in advance, either in person or by phone. If you can't get inside, it's still worth taking a look at the magnificent arcaded courtyard for which admission is free. There are a few additional exhibits for an extra charge; see p16 for more information.

⬤ DEFENSIVE WALLS

Mury Obronne; ☎ 012 422 9877; ul Pijarska; adult/concession 6/4zł; ☷ 10.30am-6pm May-Oct; ☒ 2, 4, 5, 7, 12, 13, 15

Dating to around 1300, the **Florian Gate** (Brama Floriańska) is the only gate surviving from the city's defensive walls. To the north, the **Barbican** (Barbakan) is a powerful, circular brick bastion adorned with seven turrets. This curious piece of defensive art was built around

THE TRUMPETER OF KRAKÓW

Every hour on the hour, a bugler plays a haunting melody from the Mariacka steeple. The *hejnał* is a simple five-note tune that dates back as far as the church. It is played four times, once in each direction, and was perhaps a signal of the opening and closing of the city gates. Some sources claim that bugle calls were also used to warn of fires and sound other alarms. The tune ends oddly and abruptly, its final note cut off without conclusion. Nobody knows why, but it has given rise to an intriguing legend.

The story goes that the bugler played the *hejnał* to warn of an attack by marauding Mongols back in the 13th century. As he sounded the alarm, he was shot, his heart pierced with an arrow and his warning cut short.

Alas, it is only a legend. Indeed, some claim the source of this story was an American writer, Eric Kelly, who described the tale in his 1929 children's book *The Trumpeter of Krakow*.

Never mind – Krakovians have embraced this tradition with gusto. Nowadays, a team of seven trumpeters is responsible for playing the *hejnał* every hour on the hour, around the clock. It is broadcast on Polish Radio daily at noon. See the boxed text, opposite, to meet a *hejnalista*.

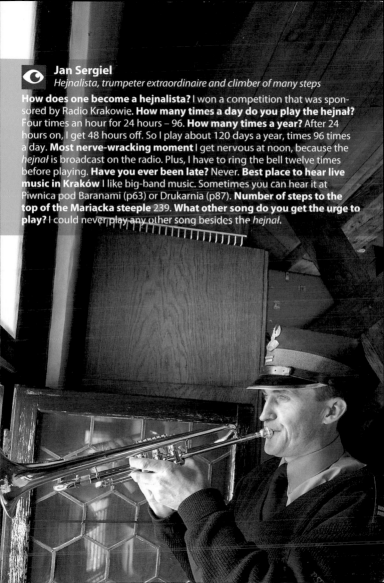

Jan Sergiel
Hejnalista, trumpeter extraordinaire and climber of many steps

How does one become a hejnalista? I won a competition that was sponsored by Radio Krakowie. **How many times a day do you play the hejnał?** Four times an hour for 24 hours – 96. **How many times a year?** After 24 hours on, I get 48 hours off. So I play about 120 days a year, times 96 times a day. **Most nerve-wracking moment** I get nervous at noon, because the *hejnał* is broadcast on the radio. Plus, I have to ring the bell twelve times before playing. **Have you ever been late?** Never. **Best place to hear live music in Kraków** I like big-band music. Sometimes you can hear it at Piwnica pod Baranami (p63) or Drukarnia (p87). **Number of steps to the top of the Mariacka steeple** 239. **What other song do you get the urge to play?** I could never play any other song besides the *hejnał*.

CRICOTEKA

Even in life it was hard to define Tadeusz Kantor, a master of both performance and visual arts, who blurred the line between genres. Poet, painter, set designer and actor, he delighted and confounded his audiences with his one-man avant-garde extravaganzas. The venue for his performances was the Cricot 2 Theatre – defunct since his death in 1990. But the **Crikoteka archive** (☎ 012 422 8332; www.cricoteka.com.pl; ul Kanonicza 5; 🕙 10am-2pm Mon & Wed-Fri, 2-6pm Tue; 🚊 6, 8, 18) documents his life work, maintaining a collection of set designs, costumes, photographs and videos. **Kantor's Atelier** (☎ 012 421 3266; ul Sienna 7/5; 🕙 10am-4pm Wed & Fri, to 6pm Tue & Thu; 🚊 6, 8, 18) is also open to the public, housing a small gallery of pieces that the artist created towards the end of his life.

1498 for additional protection; it was once connected to the gate by a narrow passage running over a moat.

🟢 DOMINICAN CHURCH OF THE HOLY TRINITY
Kościół Dominikanów Św Trójcy; ul Stolarska 12; 🚊 6, 8, 18
Originally built in the 13th century, this massive church was badly damaged by fire in 1850. Note the original 14th-century doorway at the main (western) entrance to the church. The monastery, just behind the northern wall of the church, is accessible from the street.

🟢 HIPOLIT HOUSE
Kamienica Hipolitów; ☎ 012 422 4219; www.mhk.pl; Plac Mariacki 3; adult/ concession 6/4zł, Wed free; 🕙 10am-5.30pm Wed-Sun; 🚊 1, 2, 3, 7, 8, 13, 15
This branch of the city history museum allows a glimpse of everyday burgher life from the 17th to early

19th centuries. The town house has recreated a typical home with historic interiors from these periods.

🟢 KRZYSZTOFORY PALACE
Pałac Krzysztofory; ☎ 012 619 2300; www.mhk.pl; Rynek Główny 35; adult/ concession 8/4zł, Wed free; 🕙 10am-5.30pm Wed-Sun; 🚊 2, 3, 8, 15
The palace at the corner of the Rynek Główny is the headquarters of the **History of Kraków Museum**. Once an aristocratic town house, the building now recounts the city's history from 1257 to WWII. The museum features a bit of everything related to the city's past, including armour, paintings, folk art and costumes.

🟢 MARIACKA BASILICA
Bazylika Mariacki, St Mary's Basilica; ☎ 012 422 5518; www.mariacki.com; Rynek Główny 4; church adult/concession 6/3zł, tower 5/3zł; 🕙 church 11.30am-6pm Mon-Sat, 2-6pm Sun yr-round, tower

9-11.30am & 1-5.30pm Tue, Thu & Sat May-Aug; 🚋 1, 2, 3, 7, 8, 13, 15

The twin steeples of the Mariacka Basilica tower over the Rynek Główny, acting as a geographic and historic landmark. From here the bugler plays the *hejnał* every hour, marking the time and remembering the legend of the trumpeter of Kraków (see the boxed text, p46). Enter the side door into the church, which is a veritable museum of artistic masterpieces: wall paintings by Jan Matejko; windows by Stanisław Wyspiański and Józef Mehoffer; and the gilded pentaptych altarpiece by Wit Stwosz. You can also climb to the tall tower to get up close and personal with the bugler. See also p15.

☉ MATEJKO HOUSE
Dom jana Matejki; ☎ 012 422 5926; www.muz-nar.krakow.pl; ul Floriańska 41; 🚋 2, 4, 5, 7, 12, 13, 15

Once home to Jan Matejko, this three-storey town house is now a biographical museum that displays the artwork and interiors the artist commissioned here. At the time of research, the museum was closed for a huge overhaul, but it's expected to open by the end of 2009.

☉ PALACE OF FINE ARTS
Pałac Sztuki; ☎ 012 422 6616; Plac Szczepański; 🕙 8am-6pm Mon-Fri,

10am-6pm Sat & Sun; 🚋 2, 3, 4, 8, 12, 13, 14

The centrepiece of the Art Nouveau Plac Szczepański is this elaborate edifice on its west side. An incredible frieze circles the building (product of Jacek Malczewski), while the busts on the facade honour Polish artists. The building is used for temporary art exhibits; admission price varies.

☉ PAPAL WINDOW
ul Franciszkańska 3; 🚋 6, 8, 18

When visiting Kraków, Pope John Paul II used to address his followers from this window of the Bishop's Palace, overlooking ul Franciszkańska. If you look closely, you can almost see the smiling pope waving to the people. No, really.

☉ PHARMACY MUSEUM
Muzeum Farmacji; ☎ 012 422 4284; www.muzeumfarmacji.pl; Floriańska 25; adult/concession 7/4zł; 🕙 noon-6.30pm Tue, 10am-2.30pm Wed-Sun; 🚋 2, 4, 5, 7, 12, 13, 15

Set in a beautiful historic town house, this unexpectedly fascinating museum features a 22,000-piece collection of old laboratory equipment, rare pharmaceutical instruments, glassware, stoneware, mortars, jars, barrels, medical books and documents. Several pharmacies from previous centuries have been painstakingly recreated.

● PRINCES CZARTORYSKI MUSEUM

Muzeum Książąt Czartoryskich; ☎ 012 422 5566; www.muzeum-czartoryskich .krakow.pl; ul Św Jana 19; adult/ concession 10/5zł; ✆ 10am-6pm Tue-Sat, to 4pm Sun; 🚋 2, 4, 5, 7, 12, 13, 15

Spend a few hours perusing the impressive range of European paintings, ancient artefacts and Turkish weapons. The most famous masterpieces are *Lady with an Ermine* by Leonardo da Vinci and *Landscape with the Good Samaritan* by Rembrandt, but there are loads of treasures to discover. See p20.

● TOWN HALL TOWER

Wieża Ratuszowa; ☎ 012 619 2318; adult/ concession/family 6/4/12zł; ✆ 10.30am-6pm Apr-Oct; 🚋 1, 2, 3, 7, 8, 13, 15

This tall tower is all that remains from the 15th-century town hall. In summer months, you can climb 70m to the top for a bird's-eye view of the goings-on. Nearby is the 11th-century **Church of St Adalbert** (Kościół Św Wojciecha), which predates the Rynek Główny.

● WYSPIAŃSKI MUSEUM

Muzeum Wyspiańskiego; ☎ 012 422 7021; www.muzeum.krakow.pl; ul Szczepańska 11; adult/concession 8/4zł, Thu free; ✆ 10am-6pm Tue (temporary exhibit only), to 6pm Wed-Sat, to 4pm Sun; 🚋 2, 4, 8, 12

Dedicated to the key figure of the Młoda Polska (Young Poland) movement, this museum reveals how many branches of art Stanisław Wyspiański explored.

WHAT HAVE THE AUSTRIANS EVER DONE FOR US?

When the Kingdom of Poland was dismembered at the end of the 18th century, Kraków was grabbed by the Austrians. The city's new Germanic administrators wanted to revamp the old Polish capital, making it less medieval Slavic and more imperial Habsburg. Decrepit dwellings, stenchy stalls and charmless churches were torn down; leafy lanes, brawny bridges and sanitising sewers were built up.

A main target of this reclamation project was the city's medieval wall. After five centuries, the brick barricade could no longer protect the residents from modern artillery and siege tactics. The walls, towers and grandiose gates were dismantled, and the outer moats and trenches were filled in. In its place came a new green wall, a state-of-the-art park known as **the Planty**.

Since the 1820s, the Planty has been the place to be in summer for Krakovians seeking cool cover, with the poplars overhead and lush lawns underfoot. Atop the foundations of the old city walls, it runs for more than 2 miles, encircling the architectural treasures of the Old Town. It covers more than 50 acres of flower gardens, splashing fountains, criss-crossing pathways, patriotic tributes, romantic hideaways and outdoor cafes. The Planty is the ultimate urban stroll.

A painter, poet and playwright, he was particularly renowned for his stained-glass designs, some of which are in the exhibition.

SHOP

ALHENA *Glassware*

☎ 012 421 5496; www.alhena.pl; Plac Mariacki 1; 🕑 10am-7pm Mon-Fri, 11am-3pm Sat; 🚊 1, 2, 3, 7, 8, 13, 15
This small shop sells a range of glassware from the famous Krosno factory. Most of the product line is cut glass in various colours, but there is also traditional porce-lain and more contemporary glassware.

ANDRZEJ MLECZKO GALLERY *Art Gallery*

☎ 012 421 7104; www.mleczko.pl; ul Św Jana 14; 🕑 11am-7pm Mon-Fri, 10am-3pm Sat; 🚊 1, 2, 3, 7, 8, 13, 15
Andrzej Mleczko is a popular political satirist. You might think political cartoons are language dependent but Mleczko argues that 'the funniest cartoon is still a man, a pavement and a banana peel'. Everyone can understand that.

For that souvenir with a difference: the Andrzej Mleczko Gallery

⬚ BORUNI GALLERY
Jewellery

☎ 012 423 1081; www.amber.com.pl; ul Grodzka 60; ⏰ 9am-9pm Mon-Sat, to 8pm Sun; 🚊 6, 8, 10, 18

If you are curious to know more about amber, also known as 'Baltic gold', swing by this spacious gallery to watch the informational video about the various types of amber and its production processes. A word of caution: beware the hard sell.

⬚ EMPIK *Bookstore*

☎ 012 429 4577; www.empik.com; Rynek Główny 5; ⏰ 9am-10pm; 🚊 1, 2, 3, 7, 8, 13, 15

Almost always packed, this multifloor bookstore has an excellent selection of newspapers and magazines on the ground floor, and you'll find foreign-language literature upstairs. It comes complete with a cafe, as any good megabookstore should.

⬚ GALERIA AG *Art Gallery*

☎ 012 429 5178; www.galeriaag.art.pl; Plac Dominikański 2; 🚊 6, 8, 18

This high-end gallery represents contemporary artists from all over Poland. If you can get past the stern, suited patron, you'll discover paintings and sculpture ranging from the profound to the playful.

⬚ GALERIA BUKOWSKI
Toys & Games

☎ 012 433 8855; www.galeria bukowski.pl, in Polish; ul Sienna 1; ⏰ 10am-7pm Mon-Fri, to 6pm Sat; 🚊 1, 2, 3, 7, 8, 13, 15

This unbearably cute shop specialises in *miś pluszowy* (teddy bears) of all shapes and sizes. These fuzzy-wuzzies look very sharp in their 'Poland' sweaters.

⬚ GALERIA PLAKATU
Art Gallery

Poster Gallery; ☎ 012 421 2640; www .cracowpostergallery.com; ul Stolarska 8-10; ⏰ noon-5pm Mon-Fri, 11am-4pm Sat; 🚊 6, 8, 18

Poland has always excelled in the under-appreciated art of the poster. This little gallery shows off the best of the art form, with many contemporary posters promoting exhibits and events, as well as old communist propaganda posters, both originals and reproductions.

⬚ GALERIA SKARBIEC
Jewellery

☎ 012 422 6056; ul Grodzka 35; ⏰ 10am-7pm Mon-Fri, to 3pm Sat; 🚊 6, 8, 10, 18

Colourful and contemporary jewellery fills the window of this attractive store, with necklaces, brooches, rings and earrings made with semiprecious stones. And not only amber (though there's that, too).

Leszek Żebrowski
Owner of Labirynt (p54), champion of Krakovian artists, discoverer of little-known talents and promoter of rising stars

What makes the Kraków art scene unique? Tradition. The conservative Academy of Fine Arts forces students to learn the basics before experimenting with their own styles and media; so all Kraków artists have this strong foundation, even the ones that go on to reject tradition and create something completely different. **New trends** Artists are thinking more about colour and composition, rather than themes. They are no longer interested in politics and religion. **Best collection of Polish art** National Museum (p94) for 20th century, Cloth Hall (p45) for 19th century. **Cutting-edge galleries** Starmach Gallery (p86), Bunker Sztuki (p60). **Favourite contemporary artists** Stanisław Rodzinsky, Jacek Sroka. **Favourite artist in history** Tadeusz Kantor, founder of the Crikoteka Theatre (see the boxed text, p48). **How you spend your day off** Travelling in the Pieniny mountains, listening to jazz music.

⬛ JAN FEJKIEL GALLERY
Art Gallery

☎ 012 429 1553; www.fejkielgallery
.com; ul Grodzka 65; ⏰ 11am-6pm Mon-
Fri, to 3pm Sat; 🚃 6, 8, 10, 18

Jan Fejkiel was trained as an art historian, but his gallery specialises in
contemporary prints and drawings,
with a focus on emerging artists.
This place claims the country's largest stock of contemporary graphic
art, so he's not messing around.

⬛ KRAKOWSKI KREDENS
Food & Drink

☎ 012 423 8159; www.krakowski
kredens.pl; ul Grodzka 7; ⏰ 10am-8pm
Mon-Sat, 11am-6pm Sun; 🚃 6, 8, 10, 18

Fuzzy-wuzzy heaven at Galeria Bukowski (p52)

If you love *żurek* like we love
żurek, you'll want to take some
home. Peek inside the 'Kraków
cupboard' and you'll find a jar
of this traditional sour soup, as
well as loads of edible souvenirs,
such as marinated mushrooms,
herb honey, spicy mustards and
gooseberry preserves.

⬛ LABIRYNT *Art Gallery*

☎ 012 292 6080; www.galerialabirynt
.and.pl, in Polish; ul Floriańska 36;
⏰ 10am-7pm Mon-Fri, to 3pm Sat;
🚃 1, 2, 3, 7, 8, 13, 15

Gallery owner Leszek Żebrowski
(see the boxed text, p53) works
hard to develop the Krakovian
art scene and to promote local
artists, often organising exhibits
around Poland and Europe. At his
crowded, cluttered home base,
you can see work by up-and-
coming and well-established
artists.

⬛ MY GALLERY
Jewellery & Gifts

☎ 012 431 1344; www.mygallery.pl; ul
Gołębia 1a; 🚃 6, 8, 18

This one little room has such an
eclectic assortment you could do
all your souvenir shopping here.
Choose from dramatic, nature-
inspired jewellery, handmade
scarves and sweaters, and stained-
glass sun catchers, as well as the
odd pair of soft slippers.

NEIGHBOURHOODS

OLD TOWN

◳ PUNKT *Clothing*
☎ 502 600 410; www.punkt.sklep.pl; ul Sławkówska 24; ⏲ 10am-7pm Mon-Fri, 11am-4pm Sat; ⛟ 1, 2, 3, 7, 8, 13, 15

Local designers Maja and Monika show off their funky women's fashions at their new store in the Old Town. Polish design does not get better than this – contemporary and creative, but still very classy.

◳ SALON ANTYKÓW PASJA
Antiques
☎ 012 429 1096; www.antiykwariat -pasja.pl; ul Jagiellońska 9; ⏲ 11am-7pm Mon-Fri, to 3pm Sat; ⛟ 2, 3, 8, 15

This well-established antique salon is like a minimuseum; its three rooms are stuffed with clocks, maps, paintings, lamps, sculptures and furniture. Come to think of it, it's better than a museum, because if you stumble across something you really like you can take it home.

◳ SZAMBELAN
Food & Drink
☎ 012 628 7093; www.szambelan.com .pl; ul Gołębia 2; ⏲ 10am-8pm Mon-Sat, 11am-6pm Sun; ⛟ 2, 3, 8, 15

The shelves are lined with glass beakers, filled with concoctions in all colours of the rainbow. A smiling salesperson offers a little something to cure your ills…luscious liqueurs made from local

fruits, berries and honey. There is also a wide selection of flavoured vodka and vinegar.

◳ TORUŃSKIE PIERNIKI
Food & Drink
Toruń Gingerbread; ☎ 012 431 1306; ul Grodzka 14; ⏲ 11am-7pm Mon-Fri, 10am-6pm Sat & Sun; ⛟ 6, 8, 10, 18

This sweet-smelling little shop sells a selection of delectable gingerbread products and other sweets from the town in the north of Poland. The traditional treat comes in a variety of forms, including hard baked figurines and delicious little cakes filled with marmalade.

◳ WEDEL PIJALNIA CZEKOLADY *Food & Drink*
☎ 012 429 4085; www.wedelpijalnie.pl; Rynek Główny 46; ⏲ 9am-10pm; ⛟ 1, 2, 3, 7, 8, 13, 15

The name E Wedel means only one thing: chocolate. This 'chocolate lounge' is the place to buy a box of handmade pralines to take home to your sweetheart.

🍴 EAT

🍴 AQUA E VINO
Italian €€€
☎ 012 421 2567; www.aquaevino.pl; ul Wiślna 5; ⏲ noon-11pm; ⛟ 2, 3, 8, 15; Ⓥ

Not your typical Old Town venue. This stone-vaulted cellar offers a sophisticated setting, its walls hung with oversized black-and-white photographs. The contemporary menu features inventive Veneto cuisine, including first-rate pastas, grilled meats and fresh seafood (Thursday to Sunday).

🍽 CASA DELLA PIZZA
Italian　　　　　　　€€

☎ 012 421 6498; Mały Rynek 2; 🕒 10am-late; 🚋 1, 7, 13, 24, 34; 👶
As the name would suggest, this is an amenable and unpretentious place in the Mały Rynek, away from the bulk of the tourist traffic. It has a very long menu of pizza and pasta dishes and a lovely terrace with perfect views of the Mariacka towers.

🍽 CHIMERA RESTAURANT
Polish　　　　　　€€€

☎ 012 292 1212; www.chimera.com.pl; ul Św Anny 3; 🕒 noon-11pm; 🚋 2, 3, 8, 15; 🛜
Not to be confused with the salad bar of the same name (see p59), this is a Kraków classic. The vaulted cellar is the perfect setting to sample the speciality roasted lamb, goose or game meats.

🍽 CYRANO DE BERGERAC
French　　　　　　€€€

☎ 012 411 7288; ul Sławkowska 26; 🕒 noon-midnight; 🚋 2, 4, 5, 7, 12, 13, 14; ❌
Furnished with antiques and tapestries, this award-winning

restaurant has earned a high reputation for its take on traditional French cuisine: caviar, foie gras and chateaubriand. Ooh la la.

🍽 FARINA *Seafood*　€€€

☎ 012 422 1680; www.farina.krakow .pl; ul Św Marka 16; 🕒 noon-11pm; 🚋 2, 4, 5, 7, 12, 13, 14; 🛜 👶
We don't often advise ordering seafood so far inland, but let Farina be the exception to that rule. Your server will bring over a cart showing off the creatures that are flown in from the coast, not to mention fresh flaky pike-perch

Cyrano de Bergerac: French at its most ooh la la

from local rivers. Also on offer: homemade pasta and more traditional Polish fare.

🍴 FARINELLA KUCHNIA & BAR
European €€
☎ 012 422 2121; www.farinella.pl; ul Św Anny 5; ☾ 9am-10pm; 🚃 2, 3, 8, 15; 📶
Less formal but no less delicious than her big sister Farina (opposite). Warm and welcoming, this lovely little bistro offers lighter fare such as soup, sandwiches, salads and pasta – a perfect lunch stop.

🍴 GREEN WAY
Vegetarian €
☎ 012 431 1027; www.greenway.pl; ul Mikołajska 14; ☾ 10am-10pm Mon-Fri, 11am-9pm Sat & Sun; 🚃 1, 7, 13, 24, 34; ✖ 📶 Ⓥ ♿
Primary colours and plastic interiors make this animal-free outlet feel sort of fast-foodie, but it still tastes good and – most importantly – it's still green. In this case, that means veggies galore, including loads of fresh salads, pizzas, enchiladas and more.

🍴 LA CAMPANA TRATTORIA
Italian €€€
☎ 012 430 2232; ul Kanonicza 7; ☾ noon-11pm; 🚃 6, 8, 10, 18; ✖ ♿
Not that Kraków needed another Italian restaurant, but this one boasts the city's most delightful, flower-filled courtyard setting. On a summer day, there is no better

place to sip pinot grigio and munch on antipasti.

🍴 MIÓD MALINA *Polish* €€€
☎ 012 430 0411; www.miodmalina.pl; ul Grodzka 40; ☾ noon-11pm; 🚃 6, 8, 10, 18; ✖
Country cooking at its best. Warmed by the terracotta walls and the massive stone hearth, the charmingly named 'Honey Raspberry' is a delightful place to order roasted veal with chanterelles, spareribs with plum sauce or a *pierogi* (dumpling) sampler plate. Rave reviews all around.

🍴 ORIENT EKSPRES
European €€
☎ 012 422 6672; www.orient-ekspres .krakow.pl; ul Stolarska 13; ☾ noon-11pm; 🚃 1, 7, 13, 24, 34; ♿ ♿
The stylish Orient Ekspres hearkens back to the golden age of steam. Dine in a train-car booth with vintage travel trunks scattered about. The retro decor is juxtaposed with contemporary dishes from Europe, covering just about every city from Paris to Istanbul.

🍴 POD ANIOŁAMI *Polish* €€€
Under the Angels; ☎ 012 421 3999; www.podaniolami.pl; ul Grodzka 35; ☾ 1pm-midnight; 🚃 6, 8, 10, 18
This is the quintessential Krakovian restaurant, its main dining room occupying a Gothic cellar

NEIGHBOURHOODS

OLD TOWN

from the 13th century. Heavy wood furniture, stone walls and fraying tapestries evoke the Middle Ages, as do the grilled meats cooked over a beech-wood fire.

🍴 POD KRZYŻYKIEM
Polish €€€
☎ 012 433 7010; www.podkrzyzykiem .com; Rynek Główny 39; ⏰ noon-midnight; 🚋 1, 2, 3, 7, 8, 13, 15; 🛜 ♿
Acrophobes, beware. This whimsical restaurant 'under the cross' has invented a setting in the sky, with close-up views of the Sukiennice gargoyles and Mariacka steeples,

as well as a glass floor allowing you to peer down at the Rynek Główny below. The menu is equally creative, offering a delicious new twist on Polish classics.

🍴 SZAMBELAN *Sandwiches* €
☎ 012 628 7093; www.szambelan.pl; ul Gołębia 2; ⏰ 10am-8pm Mon-Fri, 11am-6pm Sat; 🚋 6, 8, 10, 18; ✗ ♿
These fresh sandwiches and salads are a welcome change from heavy Polish fare. Choose an open-face 'toast' or a hearty ciabatta, stuffed with cured meats, cheese or vegies.

Polish country cooking at its best: Miód Malina (p57)

MILK BARS

Milk bars (bar mleczny) were designed as cheap, no-frills cafeterias, subsidised by the state during the communist era in order to provide simple, wholesome meals for the poorest citizens. The 'milk' part of the name reflects the fact that a large part of the menu was based on dairy products. Nowadays, there are plenty of simple, cafeteria-style eateries that have been updated for the modern diner on a budget. No longer solely 'milk' bars, they have menus that usually feature all your favourite traditional Polish dishes, including hot soups, goulash, stuffed cabbage, bigos (hunters' stew) and several kinds of pierogi. The following places – popular among students and other cost-conscious types – serve cheap, tasty, filling food.

Bar Grodzki (☎ 012 422 6807; www.grodzkibar.zaprasza.net; ul Grodzka 47; 🕙 9am-7pm Mon-Sat, 10am-7pm Sun; 🚊 6, 8, 10, 18; ✖) Remains true to the spirit of the bar mleczny in form and function.

Bar Smaczny (☎ 012 422 4220; ul Św Tomasza 24; 🕙 11am-7pm Mon-Fri, noon-5pm Sat; 🚊 7, 10, 19, 24, 34; V ♿) A bright simple interior with seating at picnic tables. Lunch specials and student discounts available.

Chimera Salad Bar (☎ 012 292 1212; ul Św Anny 3; 🕙 10am-10pm; 🚊 2, 3, 8, 15; ✖ 🛜 V ♿) Keep it simple: choose a big plate or a small plate, then fill it with the vegie items that look good. The covered courtyard provides a delightful setting. Don't be confused and wander into the restaurant of the same name (p56), which is significantly more expensive.

Polskie Smaki (☎ 012 429 3869; www.polskie-smaki.pl; ul Św Tomasza 5; 🕙 8am-11pm; 🚊 2, 3, 4, 12, 13, 14, 15) This place has more atmosphere than your typical milk bar, thanks to the Gothic vaulted ceiling, but the food is still straightforward and simple.

🍴 WENTZL European   €€€

☎ 012 429 5712; www.wentzl.pl;
Rynek Główny 21; 🕙 1-11pm; 🚊 1, 2, 3,
7, 8, 13, 15; 🛜

Dating back to 1792, this historic eatery is perched above the main market square. With timbered ceilings above, Oriental carpets below and fine oil paintings all around, it is certainly a spectacular setting to feast on haute cuisine such as foie gras, chanterelles in cream, and duck marinated in żubrówka (bison grass vodka).

DRINK

🍸 BLACK GALLERY Bar

☎ 012 423 0030; www.blackgallery
.krakow.pl; ul Mikołajska 24; 🕙 noon-6am Mon-Sat, 2pm-6am Sun; 🚊 7, 10,
13, 19, 24, 34

A long-standing favourite, this underground pub has a modern twist, thanks to split levels, exposed steel-frame lighting and a metallic bar. Things pick up after midnight.

NEIGHBOURHOODS

OLD TOWN

�Y CAFÉ BUNKIER *Cafe*
☎ 012 422 4021; www.bunkier.art.pl;
Plac Szczepański 3a, ☽ 9am-1am Mon-
Thu, to 2am Fri-Sun; ⓡ 2, 3, 4, 12, 13,
14, 24, 34; ♿
Bunkier Sztuki (Art Bunker) is a
cutting-edge gallery housed in a
modern building northwest of the
Rynek. Tacked onto the front is an
enormous covered terrace, which
holds this sweet open-air cafe.
Enter from the Planty.

�Y CAFÉ CAMELOT *Cafe*
☎ 012 421 0123; ul Św Tomasza 17;
☽ 9am-midnight; ⓡ 2, 3, 4, 12, 13, 14, 15
On a corner in the Old Town, this
hidden haven is a romantic destination for dates or dessert. Its cosy
rooms are cluttered with candlelit
tables and a quirky collection of
folkloric figurines. Delicious *shar-
lotka* (apple pie).

�>Y CAFÉ PHILO *Bar*
ul Św Tomasza 30; ☽ 10am-11pm Sun-
Wed, to 3am Thu-Sat; ⓡ 7, 10, 13, 19,
24, 34; 🛜
Black brick walls are lined with
well-loved books and records. Worn
leather furniture is populated by
intellectual types who look like
they might be plotting a revolution.
Chatty barstaff and clientele reas-
sure you that they are not.

☯Y CIEPLARNIA *Cocktail Bar*
☎ 012 429 2898; www.cieplarnia.krakow
.pl, in Polish; ul Bracka 15; ⓡ 6, 8, 18

It almost feels like you have been
invited into someone's living
room – the furniture is slightly
worn and the walls are cluttered
with photos. Hot drinks and jazz
music make this an ideal place to
warm up on a chilly evening.

☯Y JAMA MICHALIKA *Cafe*
☎ 012 422 1561; www.jamamichalika
.pl; ul Floriańska 45; ☽ 9am-10pm Sun-
Thu, to 11pm Fri & Sat; ⓡ 2, 3, 4, 12, 13,
14, 15; 🛜
Established in 1895, Jama Michalika is famous as the birthplace of
the Młoda Polska movement – a
hang-out for writers, painters and
other creative types in the days
of yore. The grand Art Nouveau
interior has historic appeal, but the
bored staff do not offer much in
the here and now.

☯Y NOWA PROWINCJA *Cafe*
☎ 693 770 079; www.nowaprowincja
.krakow.pl; ul Bracka 3/5; ☽ 8.30am-
11pm Mon-Sat, 9.30am-11pm Sun;
ⓡ 6, 8, 18
Gotta love this bi-level bohemian
cafe, where Kraków's coolest
cats come to drink strong coffee,
smoke cigarettes and think deep
thoughts. The original Prowincja
(next door) still has hole-in-the-
wall appeal, but head to the
more spacious new outlet to
order substantial food or sit at an
old-fashioned school desk on the
pavement.

▼ ULICA STOLARSKA
Bars & Cafes

ul Stolarska; 🚊 **1, 6, 7, 13, 18, 24, 34**
Stroll south from the Mały Rynek to investigate the city's top spot for cool cafes with people-watching potential. The street is lined (literally) with drinking venues on both sides. For quirkiness, our favourite is the **Tram Bar** (🕿 012 423 2255; www .trambar.pl; ul Stolarska 11; 🛜), which pays tribute to the city's favourite form of transportation.

▼ VINOTEKA LA BODEGA
Wine Bar

🕿 **012 425 4981; www.bodega.pl; ul Sławkowska 12;** 🕔 **10am-midnight;**
🚊 **2, 3, 4, 12, 13, 14, 15, 24;** 🛜
This straightforward and stylish venue has a small menu of Mediterranean tapas and a huge selection of wines. Shame about the gigantic TV screen.

⭐ PLAY

⭐ CIEŃ KLUB *Nightclub*
Shadow; 🕿 **012 422 2177; www.cienklub .pl; ul Św Jana 15;** 🕔 **8pm-5am Tue-Thu, to 7am Fri & Sat;** 🚊 **2, 3, 4, 12, 13, 14, 15**
One of Kraków's hottest nightspots at the time of research. What this means for you: wear your Sunday best and you *might* have the chance to get down with the upper crust or relax in the groovy garden. The crowd is attractive, as is the cavernous vaulted-cellar setting.

⭐ FRANTIC *Nightclub*
🕿 **012 423 0483; www.frantic.pl; ul Szewska 5;** 🕔 **6pm-4am Tue-Sun;** 🚊 **2, 4, 7, 8, 14;** 🛜
With two dance floors, three bars, a chill-out room and top Polish and international DJs, Frantic is regularly packed out with smart young locals. There's sniffy door selection, so don't be too scruffy.

⭐ HARRIS PIANO JAZZ BAR
Jazz

🕿 **012 421 5741; www.harris.krakow.pl, in Polish; Rynek Główny 28; admission 10-20zł;** 🕔 **9am-2am May-Oct, 1pm-2am Nov-Apr;** 🚊 **2, 3, 8, 15;** 🛜
Yet another smoky, subterranean jazz haunt, Harris has one of Kraków's most varied programs. There is jazz, blues, big band, fusion or soul music every night at 9.30pm; Mondays and Wednesdays are given over to jam sessions (free admission).

⭐ JAZZ CLUB U MUNIAKA
Jazz

🕿 **012 423 1205; ul Floriańska 3; tickets 20zł;** 🕔 **6.30pm-2am;** 🚊 **2, 3, 4, 12, 13, 14, 15**
Regarded by many as Kraków's pre-eminent jazz venue, this subterranean club was founded by the saxophonist Janusz Muniak. It attracts an impressive roll call of international artists and local groups, who play most nights at 9.30pm.

CLASSICAL MUSIC IN THE OLD TOWN

Throughout the summer, some palaces and churches in the Old Town host concerts of classical music. Sure, it's touristy, but that doesn't mean that it's not amazing music in a spectacular setting. Tickets are available at the door. Double-check the program, as your chance of hearing Vivaldi's *Four Seasons* is actually pretty high.

Bonerowski Palace (ul Św Jana 1; tickets 60zł; ☽ 7pm Wed, Fri & Sun May-Aug; ⛟ 2, 3, 4, 12, 13, 14, 15) Chopin, Chopin and more Chopin. He's Polish, you know.

Church of SS Peter & Paul (ul Grodzka 54; adult/concession 50/30zł; ☽ 4.30pm & 8pm Wed & Fri-Sun; ⛟ 6, 8, 10, 18) The afternoon concert is pianist Ireneusz Boczek, while the evening is chamber music.

Church of St Giles (ul Grodzka 67; adult/concession 50/30zł; ☽ 7pm Apr-Aug; ⛟ 3, 6, 8, 10, 18, 19, 40) Vocal and organ solo performances, as well as concerts by the Cracow Chamber Orchestra of St Maurice.

Polonia House (☎ 662 007 255; Rynek Główny 14; tickets 45zł; ☽ 7pm Tue & Fri Jun-Nov; ⛟ 2, 3, 4, 12, 13, 14, 15) 'The poet of the piano.' Yes, Chopin.

⭐ JAZZ ROCK CAFÉ *Live Music*
☎ 511 433 506; www.jazzrockcafe.pl; ul Sławkowska 12; ☽ 4pm-4am; ⛟ 2, 3, 4, 12, 13, 14, 15

Rock out almost any night of the week (from 9.30pm) in this inviting grungy bar. The place brings a post-industrial hipness to the Gothic cellar; staff are surprisingly friendly for it being so dark.

⭐ KLUB RE *Live Music*
☎ 012 431 0881; www.klubre.pl; ul Św Krzyża 4; ☽ noon-2am; ⛟ 7, 10, 13, 19, 24, 34; ⛷

You can't beat Re for its excellent line-up of live music, which features indie rock bands from all over the world, playing up close and in your face. Even if you're not into the music you'll love the shady courtyard.

⭐ LIZARD KING *Live Music*
☎ 012 422 0275; www.lizardking.pl; ul Św Tomasza 11; ☽ noon-3am; ⛷

'I am the lizard king; I can do anything', sang The Doors' Jim Morrison, an apt inspiration for this cool music club. Come for local rock bands and the occasional international act, which usually start at 9pm, from Thursday to Saturday.

⭐ PAUZA *Bar & Nightclub*
www.klubpauza.pl; ul Floriańska 18; ☽ bar 10am-midnight Mon-Sat, noon-midnight Sun, club 5pm-4am Mon-Sat, to 2am Sun; ⛟ 2, 3, 4, 12, 13, 14, 15; ⛷

Beloved for its alternative atmosphere, Pauza offers stiff drinks and heady conversation on the 1st floor (not to mention the occasional art exhibit and great window seats overlooking Floriańska).

As the night wears on, head down to the basement, where the club continues to pulse into the wee hours.

⭐ PIEC'ART *Jazz*
☎ 012 429 6425; www.piecart.pl, in Polish; ul Szewska 12; ⏱ 1pm-3am; 🚊 2, 3, 4, 8, 12, 13, 14, 15, 24
Dark and inviting, this intimate basement bar is a seductive place for a drink even when it's quiet. Several times a week, there's live acoustic jazz, which makes it all the more appealing.

⭐ PIWNICA POD BARANAMI *Cabaret*
☎ 012 421 2500; www.piwnicapod baranami.krakow.pl, in Polish; Rynek Główny; 🚊 2, 3, 4, 12, 13, 14, 15
The beer bar 'under the rams' is a legendary place, established in 1956 as a 'literary cabaret'. Nowadays the program is a bit sporadic, but the place continues to host a summer jazz festival in July and other concerts and recitals throughout the year.

⭐ RDZA *Nightclub*
☎ 600 395 541; www.rdza.pl; ul Bracka 3/5; ⏱ 7pm-6am; 🚊 6, 8, 10, 18
This is your classic Krakovian cellar, dressed up with cushy sofas, coloured lights and house music. The bouncer ensures that the dancers match the sophisticated decor.

⭐ STALOWE MAGNOLIE *Live Music*
☎ 012 422 8472; www.stalowe magnolie.com; ul Św Jana 15; ⏱ 6pm-3am; 🚊 2, 3, 4, 12, 13, 14, 15
'Steel Magnolias' is a fashionable fin-de-siècle setting to chat with friends and listen to live music. The varied program Includes indie rock, jazz and ethnically infused fusion music. Dress smartly and ring the doorbell.

⭐ STARY TEATR *Theatre*
Old Theatre; ☎ 012 422 4040; www .stary-teatr.krakow.pl; ul Jagiellońska 1; ⏱ box office 9am-5pm Mon-Fri, to 1pm Sat; 🚊 2, 3, 4, 8, 12, 13, 14, 24
Kraków's esteemed 'Old Theatre' is famous throughout the country for the quality of its productions. It presents a wide repertoire of both classic Polish and foreign plays; all shows are in Polish.

⭐ TEATR IM J SŁOWACKIEGO *Theatre*
Julius Słowacki Theatre; ☎ 012 422 4022; www.slowacki.krakow.pl; Plac Św Ducha 4; ⏱ box office 9am-5pm Mon-Fri, to 7pm performance days; 🚊 7, 10, 13, 19, 24, 34, 40
Focusing on Polish classics and large-scale productions, this important theatre is housed in an opulent building (1893) that's patterned on the Paris Opera.

WALKING TOUR
OLD TOWN INTRO

Enter the Old Town as did the kings and queens of old, through the **Barbican** (**1**; p46) and the **Florian Gate** (**2**; p46), both parts of the ancient Defensive Walls. If you're getting an early start, you can spend a few hours admiring the collection at the **Princes Czartoryski Museum** (**3**; p50) before commencing your tour. Otherwise, continue on down ul Floriańska, a pedestrian thoroughfare that was once part of the Royal Route. At the foot of Floriańska, you'll find yourself at the base of the **Mariacka Basilica** (**4**; p48); if your

timing is right, you'll hear the *hejnał* played from her steeple. Take a leisurely look around the Rynek Główny, the centre of all commercial and cultural activity in Kraków. Stroll through the **Cloth Hall** (**5**; p45) to browse the craft stalls and climb to the top of the **Town Hall Tower** (**6**; p44). At the southwest corner of the square, enter ul Św Anny and walk to the **Collegium Maius** (**7**; p46), the oldest building in Kraków. Peek into the courtyard and admire the clock, before carrying on. Turn left at ul Gołębia and follow this road southeast, then turn right and continue south on ul Bracka. Don't miss the chance to

Where kings and queens of old entered town: the imposing Barbican (p46)

duck into the **Basilica of St Francis** (8; p44) to admire the surreal stained-glass windows. Continue south on ul Grodzka, which was the final stage of the Royal Route. Go as far as ul Senacka, and from there turn south onto charming

ul Kanonicza. This will lead you right to the foot of **Wawel Hill** (9; p36). Climb to the top to see the castle grounds and cathedral, or just take in the stunning views across the river.

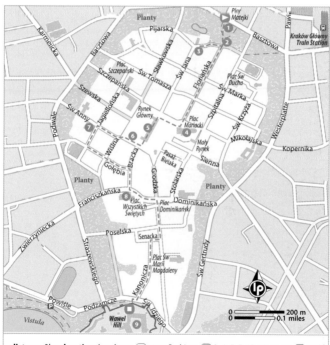

distance 2km **duration** three hours ▶ **start** Barbican 🚋 2, 4, 5, 7, 12, 13, 15, 24 ● **end** Wawel Hill 🚋 3, 6, 8, 10, 18, 19, 40

>KAZIMIERZ

Founded in 1335, Kazimierz was an independent town that rivalled Kraków for its culture and wealth. When the Jews were expelled from Kraków in 1494, they moved south and settled in a prescribed area of Kazimierz. The segregated neighbourhood contained a Christian quarter and a Jewish quarter, which were separated by a wall.

Over the centuries, the tiny Jewish quarter became a centre of Jewish culture with no equal in Poland. This cultural vibrancy vanished overnight, due to the mass deportation and extermination of the Jewish people during WWII. Today the Jewish population is estimated at about 200; only the architecture reveals that this was once a Jewish town.

KAZIMIERZ

◉ SEE

Church of St Catherine ..**1** D4
Corpus Christi Church **2** E4
Ethnographic Museum ..**3** E4
Galicia Jewish
  Museum **4** G3
Galicia Museum
  Walking Tour ....(see 27)
High Synagogue **5** F3
Isaac's Synagogue **6** F2
Jarden Tourist
  Agency ....(see 18)
Judaica Foundation **7** E3
Museum of Municipal
  Engineering **8** F4
Old Synagogue **9** G2
Pauline Church of SS Michael
  & Stanislaus **10** B4
Remuh Cemetery **11** F2
Remuh Synagogue **12** G2

◎ SHOP

Antiquarium **13** E3
Antykwariat na
  Kazimierzu ....(see 7)

Archetyp **14** F2
Błażko Kindery **15** F3
Galeria Aruaco **16** D2
Grappa.pl **17** G3
Jarden Jewish
  Bookshop **18** G1
Maruna **19** D2
Moje Marzenia **20** E2
Plac Nowy Flea
  Market **21** E2
Produkty
  Benedyktyńskie **22** E4
Raven Gallery **23** F1

🍴 EAT

Avocado **24** E2
Bagel Mama **25** E2
Dawno Temu na
  Kazimierzu **26** G1
Klezmer-Hois ....(see 27)
Kuchnia i Wino **28** F3
Młynek Café **29** E4
Momo Bar **30** D2
Pierożki U
  Vincenta **31** F3

Plac Nowy
  Okrąglak ....(see 21)
Warsztat **32** F3

▼ DRINK

Cheder ....(see 5)
Ciasteczka z
  Krakowa **33** D2
Klubokawiarnia
  Mleczarnia **34** E2
Propaganda **35** E2
Singer Café **36** F3
Zbliżenia **37** E2

⭐ PLAY

Alchemia **38** E2
Hiflyer Balon
  Widokowy **39** B4
Statek Nimfa **40** A3

Please see over for map

The heritage will be remembered, thanks in part to the artists and writers who continue to tell the tragic story. Meanwhile, Kazimierz is being reborn, as a new generation brings its own cultural vibrancy to this ever-changing neighbourhood.

SEE

CHURCH OF ST CATHERINE
Kościół Św Katarzyny; ul Augustiańska 7; 8, 10, 23, 40

The glorious Gothic Church of St Catherine was founded in 1363 and completed 35 years later, though the towers have never been built. The lofty and spacious whitewashed interior boasts an imposing, richly gilded Baroque high altar from 1634 and some very flamboyant choir stalls.

CORPUS CHRISTI CHURCH
Kościół Bożego Ciała; ul Bożego Ciała 26; 8, 10, 23, 40

Founded in 1340, Corpus Christi was the first church in Kazimierz. Its interior has been almost totally fitted out with Baroque furnishings, including the huge high altar, extraordinary massive carved stalls in the chancel and a boat-shaped pulpit. Note the surviving 15th-century stained-glass window in the sanctuary and the interesting crucifix hanging above the chancel.

Mass action inside the stunning Corpus Christi Church

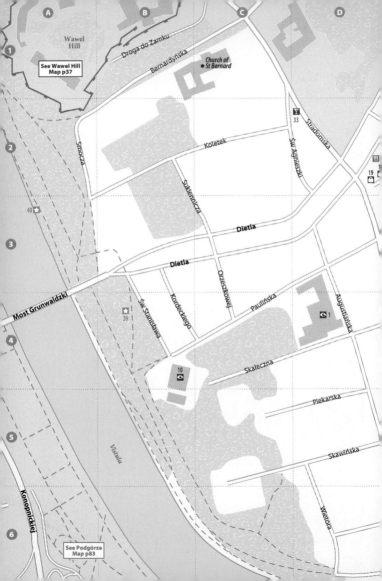

See Wawel Hill
Map p37

Wawel
Hill

Droga do Zamku

Bernardyńska

Church of
St Bernard

Koletek

Stradomska

Św Agnieszki

Dietla

Orzeszkowej

Dietla

Paulińska

Most Grunwaldzki

Św Stanisława

Kordeckiego

Skałeczna

Augustiańska

Piekarska

Skawińska

Wietora

Wisła

Konopnickiej

See Podgórze
Map p83

A   B   C   D

1   2   3   4   5   6

40

39

10

1

33

19

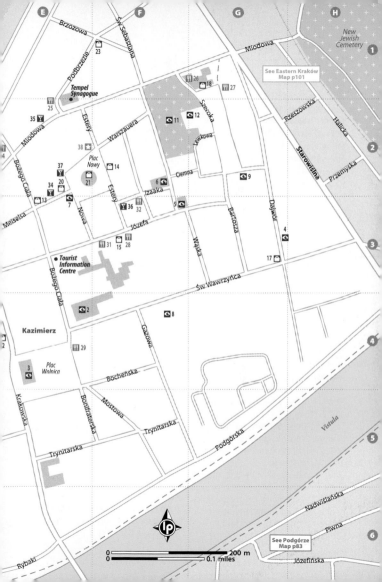

⬤ ETHNOGRAPHIC MUSEUM

Muzeum Etnograficzne; ☎ 012 430 6342; www.etnomuzeum.eu; Plac Wolnica 1; adult/concession 8/4zł, Sun free; ⏰ 11am-7pm Tue, Wed, Fri & Sat, to 9pm Thu, to 3pm Sun; 🚃 8, 10, 23, 40

The Renaissance building on Plac Wolnica was once the town hall of Kazimierz, but now it houses the Ethnographic Museum. It has one of the largest collections in Poland, including the reconstructed interiors of traditional Polish peasant cottages and workshops. There are also plenty of folk costumes, craft and trade exhibits, alongside extraordinary Nativity scenes, and religious artwork. Temporary exhibits take place at the branch around the corner at ul Krakowska 46 (adult/concession 6/3zł).

⬤ GALICIA JEWISH MUSEUM

Muzeum Galicja; ☎ 012 421 6842; www.galiciajewishmuseum.org; ul Dajwór 18; adult/child 7/5zł; ⏰ 10am-6pm; 🚃 13, 24

This excellent museum and research centre commemorates Jewish victims of the Holocaust and celebrates Jewish culture in Galicia past, present and future. The centrepiece is 'Traces of Memory', a moving photographic exhibition that depicts modern-day remnants of the once-thriving Jewish community in the southeast of the country. You can also watch testimonies of survivors on video and peruse some seminal temporary exhibits, such as 'Polish Heroes: Those Who Rescued Jews'.

⬤ HIGH SYNAGOGUE

☎ 012 430 6889; www.austeria.eu; ul Józefa 38; ⏰ 9am-6pm; 🚃 13, 24

Dating to the mid-16th century, the High Synagogue takes its name from the fact that the prayer hall was situated on the 1st floor, while the ground floor was given over to shops. Nowadays there is exhibition space in the former prayer hall, while the ground floor holds the excellent Jewish bookstore Austeria.

⬤ ISAAC'S SYNAGOGUE

Synagoga Izaaka; ☎ 012 430 5577; ul Jakuba 25, enter from ul Kupa 18; adult/concession 7/6zł; ⏰ 9am-7pm Sun-Fri; 🚃 13, 24

Kraków's largest synagogue. Completed in 1644, it was returned to the Jewish community in 1989. Inside you can see the remains of the original stuccowork and wall-painting decoration, and a photography exhibition.

⬤ JUDAICA FOUNDATION

☎ 012 430 6449; www.judaica.pl; ul Meiselsa 17; ⏰ 10am-6pm Mon-Fri, to 2pm Sat & Sun; 🚃 3, 6, 8, 10

JEWISH HERITAGE TOURS

Kazimierz is a perfect place to explore independently, uncovering its intriguing past and its vibrant present. But if you prefer to let the experts show you the ins and outs, there are a few organisations that specialise in Jewish heritage.

Galicia Museum Walking Tour (☎ 012 421 6842; www.galiciajewishmuseum.org; per person 40zł; ⏳ noon Sat) This two-hour walking tour covers historic and contemporary Kazimierz, as well as the former ghetto in Podgórze. No reservations necessary; tours depart from Klezmer-Hois (p75).

Jarden Tourist Agency (☎ 012 421 7166; www.jarden.pl; ul Szeroka 2; per person 40-80zł) The most popular option is a two-hour driving tour that visits the places made famous in *Schindler's List*. Walking tours of Kazimierz and Podgórze are also available. Advance arrangements necessary.

In a prominent spot on Plac Nowy, this Jewish culture centre hosts all kinds of exhibitions and events, from music (eg Felix Mendelssohn Music Days) to lectures (eg 'Women, Privacy and Politics') to exhibitions (such as a photo exhibition of Kazimierz from the 1950s). There is a pleasant cafe and a treasure trove of an antique store in the basement.

⊙ MUSEUM OF MUNICIPAL ENGINEERING

Muzeum Inżynierii Miejskiej; ☎ 012 421 1242; www.mimk.com.pl; Św Wawrzyńca 15; adult/child 6.50/4.50zł; ⏳ 10am-4pm Tue-Sun; 🚊 3, 6, 9, 13, 24; ♿
Tramcars and trucks fill the courtyard of this former depot while inside there's a small collection of cars and motorbikes. A room of hands-on magnetic and water experiments is sure to keep kids occupied, too.

⊙ OLD SYNAGOGUE

Stara Synagoga; ☎ 012 422 0962; www .mhk.pl; ul Szeroka 24; adult/concession 7/5zł, Mon free; ⏳ 10am-2pm Mon, 9am-5pm Tue-Sun Apr-Oct, 10am-2pm Mon, 9am-4pm Wed-Sun Nov-Mar; 🚊 13, 24
Dating back to the end of the 15th century, the aptly named Old Synagogue is in fact the oldest Jewish house of worship in the country. It now houses a branch of the Museum of the History of Kraków. The prayer hall contains the original *aron kodesh* (the niche in the eastern wall where Torah scrolls are kept) and a reconstructed *bimah* (raised platform at the centre of the synagogue where the Torah is read). Adjacent rooms are dedicated to Jewish traditions and art, while upstairs there's a photographic exhibit.

Elegant simplicity inside the Old Synagogue (p71)

PAULINE CHURCH OF SS MICHAEL & STANISLAUS

Kościół Paulinów Św Michała i Stanisława, Skałka; ☎ 012 423 0948; ul Skałeczna 15; crypt adult/concession 3/2zł; ⏰ 9am-5pm; 🚋 18, 19, 22

This most esteemed church is commonly known as the Skałka (Rock) due to its location on a once-rocky promontory. Today's mid-18th-century Baroque church is associated with Bishop Stanisław (Stanislaus) Szczepanowski, patron saint of Poland. In 1079, the bishop was beheaded by King Bolesław

Śmiały (Boleslaus the Bold): see the very tree trunk where the dirty deed was done, now in a place of honour next to the altar. Apparently the bishop's dismembered remains were tossed into a nearby pond, but the body miraculously re-formed, demonstrating the healing powers of the waters. Now the Skałka is a sort of national pantheon. The crypt underneath the church shelters the tombs of 12 eminent cultural figures, including the composer Karol Szymanowski and painters Jacek Malczewski and Stanisław Wyspiański.

REMUH SYNAGOGUE & CEMETERY

☎ 012 429 5735; ul Szeroka 40; adult/concession 5/3zł; ⏰ 9am-4pm Sun-Fri; 🚋 13, 24

Still a functioning place of worship, Remuh Synagogue was established in 1558 by a rich merchant, Israel Isserles, but it's associated with his son Rabbi Moses Isserles, a philosopher and scholar, who is buried here. Behind the synagogue, the cemetery was founded in the mid-16th century. It was closed for burials in the late 18th century, when a new and larger graveyard was established (see p102). The tombstones have been meticulously restored since WWII, making the place one of the best-preserved Renaissance Jewish cemeteries anywhere in Europe.

🛍 SHOP

🏛 ANTIQUARIUM *Antiques*
☎ 601 860 761; ul Meiselsa 20; 🕙 9am-5pm Mon-Fri, to 3pm Sat & Sun; 🚊 3, 6, 8, 10

Two rooms are packed to the gills with cuckoo clocks, silverware, ornate wood furniture and porcelain ware. We're sure there is loads of good stuff in here but it's up to you to find it.

🏛 ANTYKWARIAT NA KAZIMIERZU *Antiques*
Antiques in Kazimierz; ☎ 012 292 6153; ul Meiselsa 17; 🕙 10am-5pm Mon-Fri, to 2pm Sat & Sun; 🚊 3, 6, 8, 10

In the basement of the Judaica Foundation (p70), this Aladdin's cave is a jumble of antique china, glass, paintings, books and other assorted schlock.

🏛 BŁAŻKO KINDERY *Jewellery*
☎ 012 430 6731; ul Józefa 11; 🕙 11am-7pm Mon-Fri, to 3pm Sat; 🚊 6, 8, 10

The eye-catching creations of Grzegorz Błażko are on display in this little shop, including his unique range of chequered enamel rings, pendants, bracelets, earrings and cufflinks. Most are silver.

🏛 GRAPPA.PL *Sportswear*
☎ 012 421 1778; www.grappa.pl, in Polish; ul Dajwór 25; 🕙 10.04am-6.04pm Mon-Fri, to 2.05pm Sat; 🚊 13, 24

If you're going to play the game, you'll need the kit. This affable and helpful shop stocks everything you'll need to start hiking, trekking or climbing. We can't explain the hours of operation – perhaps a four-minute snooze button.

YOU GOTTA HAVE ART

Artists and creative types have flocked to Kazimierz, turning it into Kraków's most bohemian borough. A short stroll down ul Józefa will allow art-lovers to explore a dozen different denizens of artistry and creativity, while others are scattered around town, including the following:

Archetyp (☎ 012 421 0465; www.archetyp.art.pl; ul Estery 10) Naively painted wooden sculptures depicting saints and devils.

Galeria Aruaco (☎ 602 396 230; www.etniczne.com; ul Miodowa 4) Funky, chunky jewellery that is reminiscent of tropical places.

Maruna (☎ 609 916 199; www.maruna.pl; ul Miodowa 2; 🕙 11am-7pm Mon-Sat, to 3pm Sun) Cute, clever jewellery, clothing and toys – all of it made from recycled stuff.

Raven Gallery (☎ 012 431 1129; www.raven.krakow.pl; ul Brzozowa 7; 🕙 11am-6pm Mon-Fri, to 3pm Sat) Specialising in Art Deco gems, this place displays paintings, sculpture and furniture from the 19th century to present day.

📷 JARDEN JEWISH BOOKSHOP *Bookstore*

☎ 012 421 7166; www.jarden.pl; ul Szeroka 2; 🕙 9am-6pm Mon-Fri, 10am-6pm Sat & Sun; 🚊 3, 9, 11, 13, 24
This small bookshop is dedicated to Kraków's Jewish heritage, with numerous titles on Jewish history, culture, cuisine, legends and more, in English and other languages. It also sells guidebooks to Kazimierz and runs tours of sites of Jewish interest (see the boxed text, p71).

📷 MOJE MARZENIA *Clothing*

My Dream; ☎ 790 466 103; www.lnianemarzenie.pl; ul Meiselsa 22; 🕙 11am-6pm Tue-Fri, to 2pm Sat & Sun; 🚊 3, 6, 8, 10

You might think you are dreaming too, ladies. Natural materials and subtly sexy styles characterise the designs that are on display at this tiny boutique. Linen dresses, pants and shirts, as well as handmade jewellery and fabulous sunhats.

📷 PLAC NOWY *Market*

Plac Nowy; 🕙 from 6am; 🚊 3, 6, 8, 10
Sometimes called the Jewish Market, this flea market is best on Saturday and Sunday mornings, when it's crammed with stalls selling everything from clothing to comic books. On other days, you'll find scattered tables with fresh produce, antiques, and Judaism- and communism-related souvenirs.

Antykwariat na Kazimierzu (p73): dig for your treasure in this Aladdin's cave

PRODUKTY BENEDYKTYŃSKIE *Food & Drink*

Benedictine Products; ☎ 012 422 0216; ul Krakowska 29; ⏰ 9am-6pm Mon-Fri, to 3pm Sat; 🚋 8, 10, 23, 40

The Benedictine monks are nothing if not industrious. Here you can buy cheese, wine, cookies, honey…all the goodies that are produced by the holy men up the river in Tyniec (see the boxed text, p98), as well as some products from monasteries further afield.

🍽 EAT

🍽 AVOCADO *European* €€

☎ 012 422 0486; www.restoavocado .pl; ul Bożego Ciała 1; ⏰ 11am-11pm; 🚋 18, 19, 22; 📶 ♿

Believe it or not, there is not an ounce of guacamole on this menu. Rather, the sophisticated European fare includes delights such as roasted lamb in chèvre sauce or grilled salmon with strawberry salsa. Take a seat on the lovely patio, or retreat indoors into contemporary chic.

🍽 BAGEL MAMA *Bagels* €

☎ 012 431 1942; www.bagelmama .com; ul Podbrzezie 2; ⏰ 10am-7pm Tue-Sun; 🚋 18, 19, 22; ✖

How clever of someone to think of selling bagels in the Jewish quarter. Whether you are a bagel traditionalist (lox and cream cheese) or a bagel innovator (warm brie and tomato), you'll find something you

like. For some reason, there are also burritos on the menu.

🍽 DAWNO TEMU NA KAZIMIERZU *Jewish* €€

Once Upon a Time in Kazimierz; ☎ 012 421 2117; ul Szeroka 17; ⏰ 10am-midnight; 🚋 13, 24

As you approach this restaurant from ul Miodowa, you'll see signs from yesteryear: Chajim Kohan's General Store, Szymon Kac Tailor, Nowak Grocery. The shop windows still display the goods from times gone by. Inside, the quaint restaurant serves decent Polish-Jewish food, though you're really coming for the historic atmosphere.

🍽 KLEZMER-HOIS *Jewish* €€

☎ 012 411 1245; www.klezmer.pl; ul Szeroka 6; ⏰ 10am-9.30pm; 🚋 13, 24

More than any other restaurant, Klezmer-Hois evokes pre-war Kazimierz, with its tables covered in lace, and artwork inspired by the *shtetl* (Jewish town). Warm up with a bowl of delicious soup invented by Yankiel the Innkeeper of Berdytchov. In the evenings, folks gather for concerts of traditional Jewish music (8pm).

🍽 KUCHNIA I WINO *European* €€

☎ 012 430 6710; www.kuchniaiwino.eu; ul Józefa 13; ⏰ noon-10pm; 🚋 3, 6, 8, 10

The name, 'Cuisine and Wine', may not suggest this bistro has a

STREET FOOD

The charming, round, brick building at the centre of Plac Nowy is the **Okrąglak**, or rotunda, built in 1900 as a marketplace. These days, the rotunda serves the important function of a late-night food court. The narrow windows are portals to Polish fast-food joints that stay open into the wee hours to cater to carousers from the local clubs and pubs.

The late-night nosh of choice? That would be the *zapiekanka*, a sort of baguette pizza that is the speciality of Plac Nowy. The idea is simple: it's a half of a baguette, topped with cheese, ham and mushrooms. Other varieties are available (the Hawaiian has ham and pineapple), but nothing beats the classic. It's a cheap filling snack that tastes especially delicious after midnight. Indeed, there may be no reason to eat it before midnight. There is certainly no reason to eat it anyplace other than Plac Nowy.

Beware: *zapiekanka* is typically topped with ketchup. If this sounds disgusting, make sure you order yours without (technically *bez sosa pomidorowego*, but 'no ketchup' will work).

lot of imagination, however, the delightfully inspired Mediterranean menu is unusual in Kraków, featuring handmade pasta and fresh seafood. It's hard to resist the lovely garden setting, while the interior, with its sky-painted ceiling and Tuscan tones, is also inviting.

🍴 MŁYNEK CAFÉ *Vegetarian* €
☎ 012 430 6202; www.cafemlynek.pl; Plac Wolnica 7; 🚋 8, 10, 23, 40; 🛜 Ⓥ
This vegetarian cafe is the perfect pit stop on the 'other' side of Kazimierz. It offers delectable, animal-free soups and sandwiches; occasional concerts, poetry readings and art exhibits; a collection of typewriters and coffee grinders to admire; and outdoor seating overlooking the square. What's not to like?

🍴 MOMO BAR *Vegetarian* €
☎ 609 685 775; ul Dietla 49; 🕙 11am-8pm; 🚋 18, 19, 22; ⊠ ⓐ Ⓥ
Vegans will cross the doorstep of this restaurant with relief – the majority of the menu items are completely animal-free. The space is decorated with Indian craft pieces, and serves up subcontinental soups, stuffed pancakes and rice dishes, with a great range of cakes. Go for the namesake *momos* (Tibetan dumplings).

🍴 PIEROŻKI U VINCENTA *Polish* €
☎ 012 430 6834; ul Józefa 11; 🕙 noon-10pm Sun-Thu, to 11pm Fri & Sat; 🚋 3, 6, 8, 10; ⊠ Ⓥ
There are only four tables in this place, but there are about 40 kinds

of dumplings on the menu; sweet and savoury, classic and creative. Maybe you thought you were tired of *pierogi*, but Vincent will convince you to eat one more plate!

🍴 WARSZTAT *Italian* €€
☎ 012 430 1451; ul Izaaka 3; ⏰ 10am-10pm; 🚊 3, 6, 8, 10; **V**

Takes the concept of 'piano bar' to a whole new level. Horns, harps and accordions adorn the walls, while the centrepiece is a piano submerged into the floor. Delicious pizzas, pastas and salads constitute the bulk of the menu.

🍸 DRINK

🍸 CHEDER *Cafe*
☎ 012 431 1517; www.cheder.pl; ul Józefa 36; ⏰ 11am-10pm Tue-Sun; 🚊 13, 24

Unlike most of the other Jewish-themed places in Kazimierz, this one aims to entertain *and* educate. Named after a traditional Hebrew school, the cafe offers access to a decent library in Polish and English, regular readings and films, as well as real Israeli coffee, brewed in a traditional Turkish copper pot with cinnamon and cardamom.

Get things all stitched up at the Singer Café (p78)

☿ CIASTECZKA Z KRAKOWA
Cafe

Cookie from Kraków; ☎ 012 428 2890; ul Stradomska 19; ⏱ 9am-9pm Mon-Sat, 10am-8pm Sun

Halfway between Kazimierz and the Old Town, this is a perfectly pleasant place to stop for a coffee or tea, but nobody leaves without sampling the goods from the cookie counter. C is for Ciasteczka.

☿ KLUBOKAWIARNIA MLECZARNIA *Cafe*

☎ 012 421 8532; www.mle.pl; ul Meiselsa 20; ⏱ 10am-midnight; 🚋 3, 6, 8, 10; 📶

Wins the prize for best courtyard cafe. Shady trees and blooming roses make this place tops for a sunny-day drink. If it's rainy, never fear, for the cafe is warm and cosy, with crowded bookshelves and portrait-covered walls. Self service.

☿ PROPAGANDA *Bar*

☎ 012 292 0402; ul Miodowa 20; ⏱ 11am-3am Sun-Thu, to 5am Fri & Sat; 🚋 18, 19, 22

This is another one of those places full of communist nostalgia, but so real are the banners and mementoes that we almost started singing the 'Internationale'. Killer cocktails.

☿ SINGER CAFÉ *Club-Cafe*

☎ 012 292 0622; ul Estery 20; ⏱ 9am-4am Sun-Thu, to 5am Fri & Sat; 🚋 3, 6, 8, 10; 📶

Louche hang-out of choice among the Kazimierz cognoscenti, this bar pays tribute to the sewing machine that was once produced here. By day, it's an atmospheric, antique-filled cafe, where patrons sit at sewing machines and sip cappuccinos. By night, they turn up the music and the place hums until dawn.

☿ ZBLIŻENIA *Cafe*

☎ 012 430 0138; Plac Nowy 71/2; ⏱ 9am-midnight; 🚋 3, 6, 8, 10; 📶 ♿

Tucked into the corner of Plac Nowy, it's easy to miss this place, but don't pass it by. Krakovians rave about this luscious, laid-back little bar. It's hip enough to impress a date, but friendly enough that you want to return again and again. Decent food, sweet garden.

⭐ PLAY

⭐ ALCHEMIA *Live Music*

☎ 012 421 2200; www.alchemia.com.pl; ul Estery 5; concerts 30-50zł; ⏱ 9am-3am; 🚋 3, 6, 8, 10; ♿

Decked out with the usual retro Kazimierz knick-knackery, Alchemia offers multiple rooms for drinking and watching the activity on Plac Nowy. Most importantly, the grungy, arcaded basement hosts the best line-ups of live music acts in town, including jazz, blues and pop.

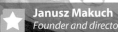

Janusz Makuch
Founder and director of the Jewish Culture Festival (p18);
lover of Jewish music, food and fun; celebrator of contemporary culture

Favourite part of the festival I am most proud of our workshops, taught by eminent Jewish cultural figures and scholars. I also love the music. **Best Jewish music in Kraków** The Bester Quartet (www.besterquartet.com) plays every month at Café Camelot (p60). Kroke (www.kroke.krakow.pl), which means 'Kraków' in Yiddish, is an interesting local band that combines both klezmer and Sephardic music. You can occasionally see the legendary Leopold Kozłowski right up the street at Klezmer-Hois (p75). **Best Jewish food** This year at the festival we are offering two workshops on Jewish and Sephardic cuisine! At other times, Klezmer-Hois (p75) is probably the best. Cheder (p77) is the only place serving authentic coffee brewed in the Israeli style. **Organisations working to preserve and promote Jewish culture in Kraków** Galicia Jewish Museum (p70), Austeria publishing house (p70), Judaica Foundation (p70).

⭐ HIFLYER BALON WIDOKOWY *Lookout*

Hiflyer Viewing Balloon; ☎ 500 444 545; www.hiflyer.pl; most Grunwaldzki; adult/concession 35/18zł; 🕐 **10am-8pm Apr-Sep;** 🚌 **18, 19, 22;** ♿

For fabulous views of Wawel Castle and the Old Town, it's hard to beat the Hiflyer hot-air balloon. Moored along the Vistula (Wisła) River, near the Grunwald Bridge, the enormous balloon takes passengers for a 15-minute float 150m over the city. On a clear day you can see the Tatras.

⭐ STATEK NIMFA *River Cruise*

☎ **012 422 0855; www.statek.krakow .pl; Wawel pier; 1hr cruise adult/ concession 15/12zł, 3hr cruise 30/25zł;** 🕐 **10am-6pm;** 🚌 **18, 19, 22**

The pleasure boat *Nimfa* cruises along the Vistula River, departing from the pier below Wawel Castle, and motoring past sights such as Kościuszko Mound, Skałka and Plac Bohaterów Getta, with up-close views of all six bridges. The three-hour tour goes all the way to Tyniec.

WALKING TOUR
KAZIMIERZ CRUISE

Beginning at the base of Wawel Hill, walk south along the river bank. Just past the Grundwald Bridge you'll see the **Pauline Church of SS Michael & Stanislaus** (**1**; p72), commonly known as the Skałka. Across the field, about 250m east sits the Gothic **Church of St Catherine** (**2**; p67), one of the city's most monumental churches. Continue east on ul Skałeczna, turn right into ul Krakowska, and you'll see the former town hall of Kazimierz, which now houses the **Ethnographic Museum** (**3**; p70). In the northeastern corner of Plac Wolnica is **Corpus Christi Church** (**4**; p67), which served for a long time as the town's parish church.

From here, walk east along ul Św Wawrzyńca for 500m to the Jewish quarter. Turn left at ul Wąska and walk one block north. In front of you is the **High Synagogue** (**5**; p70), with an excellent Jewish bookstore on the ground floor. About 100m northwest is **Isaac's Synagogue** (**6**; p70), which sometimes hosts exhibitions.

Now wind your way through the narrow decrepit streets until you end up at ul Szeroka, traditionally the centre of the Jewish quarter. Although *ulica Szeroka* means 'wide street', it looks more like an elongated square. Near the northern end is the **Remuh Synagogue** (**7**; p72), the only synagogue that is still in regular use, and the Renaissance cemetery behind it. At the southern end is the fine **Old Synagogue** (**8**; p71), which now contains a branch of the Museum of the History of Kraków.

Make sure you save time for the **Galicia Museum** (**9**; p67), which is one block east on ul Dajwór. Northeast of the Jewish quarter and behind the railway bridge is the **New**

Jewish Cemetery (**10**; p102), the only burial place for Jews now in use in Kraków. You can return to the Old Town by tram from ul Starowiślna, or walk south along the same street and over the bridge to the suburb of Podgórze.

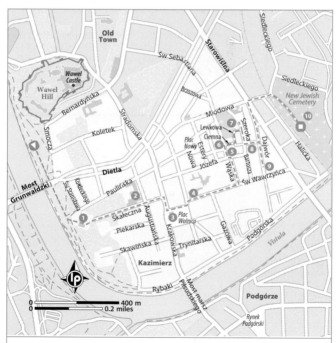

distance 3km **duration** three to four hours ▶ **start** most Grunwaldzki 🚊 18, 19, 22 ● **end** ul Starowiślna 🚊 9, 11, 13, 24, 34

>PODGÓRZE

This working-class suburb would pique the curiosity of few travellers if it wasn't for the notorious role it played during WWII. It was here that the Nazis herded some 15,000 Jews into a ghetto and then emptied it by way of deportations to concentration camps. A smattering of sites recall these events – the eerie Plac Zgody, now named for the 'heroes of the ghetto'; the famed factory of Oskar Schindler, where many lives were saved; and the site of the former Płaszów concentration camp, a short distance to the southwest.

Today Podgórze is an intriguing mix. It's a mostly industrial district with a tragic history, which makes it attractive for artistic creative types in search of the next best thing. That explains why Podgórze is the unlikely home of Kraków's most inventive art gallery. It also explains the existence of a few cool clubs and cafes – not many, but enough to prove that the place really is 'up and coming'.

PODGÓRZE

◉ SEE
Church of St Benedict **1** E3
Ghetto Wall **2** E2
Krakus Mound **3** F4
Manggha Centre of Japanese
   Art & Technology **4** B1
Pharmacy Under the
   Eagle **5** E2
Plac Bohaterów Getta ...**6** E2
Płaszów Camp **7** F4
Schindler's Factory **8** F2

⬛ SHOP
Starmach Gallery **9** E3

🍴 EAT
Delecta **10** E2
Pod Lwem **11** D2
With Fire & Sword **12** C3

▾ DRINK
Café Rękawka **13** D2
Cava ....(see 14)

★ PLAY
Drukarnia 14 D2

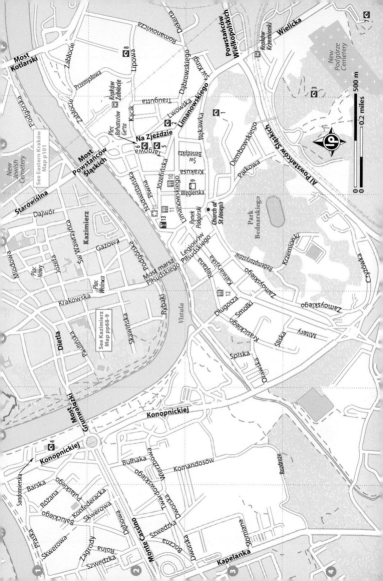

Most Kotlarski

Zabłocie

Przemysłowa

Zabłocie

See Eastern Kraków Map p101

New Jewish Cemetery

Most Powstańców Śląskich

Starowiślna

Dajwór

Kazimierz

Podgórska

Gazowa

Sw Wawrzyńca

Plac Nowy

Józefa

Józefa

Miodowa

Krakowska

Dietla

Plac Wolnica

See Kazimierz Map pp68-9

Skawińska

Rybaki

Most marsz Piłsudskiego

Most Piłsudskiego

Vistula

Podgórska

Nadwiślańska

Piwna

Josefińska

Nadwiślańska

Limanowskiego

Rynek Podgórski

Church of St Joseph

Węgierska

Sw Benedykta

Krakusa

Targowa

Na Zjeżdzie

Lwowska

Limanowskiego

Rękawka

Dąbrowskiego

Romanowicza

Dekerta

Lipowa

Kącik

Traugutta

Legionów

Piłsudskiego

Parkowa

Dembowskiego

Al Powstańców Śląskich

Powstańców Wielkopolskich

Wielicka

Kraków Krzemionki

New Podgórze Cemetery

Park Bednarskiego

Redemptorystów

Zamoyskiego

Kremionki

Czyżówka

Zamoyskiego

Kalwaryjska

Rejtana

Zamoyskiego

Krasickiego

Długosza

Smolki

Kraszewskiego

Śliska

Spiska

Mitery

Orawska

Most Grunwaldzki

Konopnickiej

Konopnickiej

Bałuckiego

Sandomierska

Barska

Różana

Pułaskiego

Konfederacka

Skwerowa

Ogrody

Rolna

Praska

Skwerowa

Szwedzka

Monte Cassino

Dębowa

Twardowskiego

Dworskie

Bułhaka

Wierzbowa

Komandosów

Rozdroże

Szwedzka

Boczna

Dworska

Słomiane

Kapelanka

500 m

0.2 miles

0

👁 SEE

👁 CHURCH OF ST BENEDICT

Kościółek Św Benedykta; ul Rękawka;
🚋 **3, 6, 9, 13, 24, 34**

Tucked into a wooded hillside above Podgórze, this mysterious little church is one of the oldest in Kraków. Historians are not certain of its origin, though archaeologists estimate that it was built in the 12th century. Although the interior has been restored, the church is open only once a year on the first Tuesday after Easter, when the spring festival of Rękawka (see the boxed text, p25) is celebrated.

👁 KRAKUS MOUND

Kopiec Krakusa; al Pod Kopcem;
🕐 **dawn-dusk;** 🚋 **3, 6, 9, 13, 24, 34**

Nobody knows the exact origins of the 16m mound that towers over Podgórze. According to legend, it was the burial site of the city's founder, Prince Krak. Excavations in the 1930s could not confirm this story, but they did discover artefacts dating to the 7th century. The mysterious mound offers 360° of panoramic views, including the Old Town, Kazimierz, Nowa Huta and Płaszów.

WHOEVER SAVES ONE LIFE, SAVES THE WORLD ENTIRE

At Jerusalem's Yad Vashem, a museum dedicated to the Holocaust, there is a row of trees called the 'Avenue of the Righteous Among Nations'. The trees represent some of the 21,300-odd Gentiles (non-Jews) who risked their own lives to save Jews during the Holocaust. Among those so honoured is Oskar Schindler, a heavy-drinking profiteer and something of an antihero. He originally saved the lives of Jews because he needed their cheap labour at his enamelware factory (see p86), though he later used his connections and paid bribes to keep his employees from being shipped off to concentration camps. Schindler is probably the best known of the so-called 'righteous Gentiles' thanks to the book by Thomas Keneally, *Schindler's Ark* (1982), and Steven Spielberg's mega-hit film *Schindler's List* (1993).

Another 'righteous Gentile' was pharmacist Tadeusz Pankiewicz, who was allowed to operate the **Pharmacy Under the Eagle** (opposite) in the ghetto until the final deportation. Pankiewicz dispensed medicines (often without charge), carried news from the outside world and even allowed use of the establishment as a safe house on occasion. His harrowing memoir, *The Cracow Ghetto Pharmacy*, describes many of these deeds without bravado or boast, and provides an eyewitness account of the ghetto's short and tragic history from beginning to liquidation.

These are the best known and most celebrated examples, but there are some 6000 Poles honoured in Jerusalem. Some of them are still living in Kraków. Learn about these unsung heroes at the **Galicia Jewish Museum** (p70) in Kazimierz. The exhibit 'Polish Heroes: Those Who Rescued Jews' focuses on the lives and deeds of a few Kraków residents who did what they could to save a life. As it says in the Talmud, 'Whoever saves one life, saves the world entire'.

MANGGHA CENTRE OF JAPANESE ART & TECHNOLOGY

☎ 012 267 2703; www.manggha .krakow.pl; ul Konopnickiej 26; adult/ concession 15/10zł, Tue free; ⏰ 10am-6pm Tue-Sun Sep-May, 10am-8pm Tue-Sun Jun-Aug; 🚃 18, 19, 22

Lying on the right bank of the Vistula (Wisła) River diagonally opposite Wawel Hill, this impressive project was the brainchild of the Polish film director Andrzej Wajda, who donated his Kyoto Prize money to fund a permanent home for the National Museum's extensive Japanese collection. The collection includes art, ceramics, weapons, fabrics, scrolls, woodcuts and comics. Most of the 7000 pieces were assembled by Feliks Jasieński (1861–1929), an avid traveller, art collector, literary critic and essayist, known by his pen name of Manggha.

PHARMACY UNDER THE EAGLE

Apteka Pod Orłem; Plac Bohaterów Getta 18; ☎ 012 656 5625; adult/concession 5/4zł; ⏰ 10am-2pm Mon, 9.30am-5pm Tue-Sat; 🚃 9, 11, 13, 24, 34

Operated by Tadeusz Pankiewicz until the final deportation, the ghetto's only pharmacy was a sort of safe haven, where Jews could receive medical care and news from the outside world. It's now a museum that recalls ghetto events and the pharmacist's heroic deeds. See also the boxed text, opposite.

PLAC BOHATERÓW GETTA

🚃 9, 11, 13, 24, 34

The centre of the Jewish ghetto was Plac Zgody, now named after the 'heroes of the ghetto'. This was the point of departure for thousands of Jews who boarded the waiting trains to the various camps. Today it is marked with a memorial by Kraków architects Piotr Lewicki and Kazimierz Latak consisting of 70 eerily empty chairs, which represent furniture and other remnants discarded by the deportees. Just south of the

Shadows of the past: moving memorial to ghetto victims at Plac Bohaterów Getta

square on ul Lwowska is a remaining piece of the **ghetto wall** with a plaque marking the site.

SCHINDLER'S FACTORY
Fabryka Schindlera; ☎ 012 257 1017; www.mhk.pl; ul Lipowa 4; ⏰ 10am-5.30pm Tue-Sun; 🚃 125, 425

The massive enamelware factory (made famous by Steven Spielberg) was where Oskar Schindler employed thousands of Jewish prisoners – and eventually saved many of their lives. The factory is scheduled to open in 2009 as an interactive, multimedia museum of WWII history. The long-awaited, highly anticipated museum will feature exhibits on the Nazi invasion of Poland, daily life in the ghetto and the Płaszów Camp, as well as a re-creation of Schindler's office. The thought-provoking 'room of choices' encourages visitors to consider the difficult judgments that every person had to make during the war.

🛍 SHOP
🛍 STARMACH GALLERY
Art Gallery
☎ 012 656 4317; www.starmach.com.pl; ul Węgierska 5; ⏰ 11am-6pm Mon-Fri; 🚃 3, 6, 11, 23

Starmach is among the city's most prestigious galleries of contemporary painting and sculpture, exhibiting both emerging and established Polish artists. The striking modern gallery is housed in the former Jewish Zucher prayer house, a 19th-century neo-Gothic brick beauty.

🍴 EAT
🍴 DELECTA *Pizzeria*   €€
☎ 012 423 5001; www.restauracja-delecta.pl; ul Limanowskigo 11; ⏰ 11am-10pm Sun-Thu, to 11pm Fri & Sat; 🚃 3, 6, 11, 23

There are not a huge number of restaurants in Podgórze, but there is pizza. Tasty pies come with all kinds of toppings: some are authentic while others are inventive (the Delecta speciality pizza

Contemporary sculpture at Starmach Gallery

features ham, bacon and corn kernels). The place goes all out for Italy, with its Tuscan-sun decor.

🍴 POD LWEM *European* €
☎ 519 374 737; www.podlwem.malo polska.pl; ul Józefińska 4; ⏰ 8am-10pm Mon-Sat, 9am-10pm Sun; 🚋 3, 6, 11, 23
Named after the evocative bas-relief on its facade, this cute cafe 'under the lion' is a fine place for a tasty breakfast or a light lunch. Specialities such as grilled eggplant and chicken in mustard-cream sauce are a nice change of pace from *bigos* (stew) and *pierogi*.

🍴 WITH FIRE & SWORD *Polish* €€€
Ogniem i Mieczem; ☎ 012 656 2328; www.ogniemimieczem.pl; Plac Serkowsk-iego 7; ⏰ noon-midnight Mon-Sat, to 9.30pm Sun; 🚋 8, 10, 11, 23; ♿
Named after the historical novel by Henry Sienkiewicz, this dark, atmospheric restaurant re-creates the Poland of yesteryear. The wood interior is made even more rustic with animal pelts and a roaring fire. The menu features well-researched old-time recipes, such as the succulent roasted pig that comes stuffed with fruit.

🍸 DRINK
🍸 CAFE RĘKAWKA *Cafe*
☎ 012 296 2002; ul Brodzinskiego 4b; ⏰ 8am-10pm; 🚋 3, 6, 11, 23

The smell of fresh-brewed java and the sounds of jazz music entice you into this sweet sanctuary. It's a funny mismatch of burlap coffee bags, lace curtains and leafy plants, creating the perfect atmosphere to sink into a comfortably worn arm-chair and warm up with a cuppa.

🍸 CAVA *Wine Bar*
☎ 012 656 7456; www.cafecava.pl; ul Nadwiślańska 1; ⏰ 9am-10pm Sun-Thu, to midnight Fri & Sat; 🚋 3, 6, 11, 23; 📶
In up-and-coming Podgórze, one does not expect to see such a chic little wine bar, but here it is, com-plete with post-industrial decor and spiffy waitstaff. Come for cappuc-cino or cava (duh). If you're hungry, there are sophisticated, Med-style tapas listed on the slate board.

⭐ PLAY
⭐ DRUKARNIA
Live Music & Nightclub
☎ 012 656 6560; www.drukarnia -podgorze.pl; ul Nadwiślańska 1; ⏰ 10am-last guest; 🚋 3, 6, 11, 23; 📶 ♿
Old typewriters and newsprint wallpaper evoke the namesake 'printhouse', creating an arty atmosphere at this riverside venue. Upstairs, there are two spacious bars and pavement seating; down-stairs is where the music goes down (live music on Wednesday and Thursday, dance parties on Friday and Saturday).

DETOUR: PŁASZÓW CAMP

Not much remains from this Nazi concentration camp, where thousands of prisoners died from hard labour, hunger, disease and execution. Built on the site of a Jewish cemetery, it operated as a labour camp in 1942 and was converted to a concentration camp in January 1944. Nowadays, the vast site consists of rolling hills and unkempt fields, a strangely peaceful setting that belies the tragedy that took place here.

The only existent camp buildings are the **Grey House** (ul Jerozelimska 3), which held prison and torture cells. On a nearby residential street is an **abandoned house** (ul Heltmana 22) that was the home of the notoriously brutal SS commandant Amon Goeth.

The overgrown grounds contain some scattered monuments, including the moving **Memorial of Ripped-Out Hearts** in the far south. In the northern part of the grounds, you can find a few **gravestones** – the only evidence of the Jewish cemetery that occupied this spot before the war.

To reach the camp, take any tram bound for Podgórze (No 3, 6, 9, 13, 24 or 34) and get off at Dworcowa. Otherwise, you can walk south from Krakus Mound: cut between the cemetery and the quarry and follow the path into the camp grounds.

WALKING TOUR
EXPLORING PODGÓRZE

Undoubtedly, Schindler's Factory (p86) and Plac Bohaterów Getta (p85) are the most visited attractions in Podgórze. But this neighbourhood on the edge has even more to offer, especially for travellers who are willing to wander off the beaten track. Start at the Rynek Podgórski, the district's central square that is dominated by the majestic **Church of St Joseph (1)**. Built in 1905, the neo-Gothic facade is festooned with gargoyles and crowned with a beautiful clock tower. From the square, stroll east along ul Rękawka, taking a detour to stop into the **Starmach Gallery (2**; p86).

Follow the footpath that leads up the hill to the ancient **Church of St Benedict (3**; p84), one of the city's oldest and most mysterious churches. Nearby is the abandoned **St Benedict Fort (4)**, which was built in the 1850s to defend the bridge over the Vistula River. To the south is the **Old Podgórze Cemetery (5)**, an 18th-century burial ground that is the final resting place of many artists and heroes.

South of the cemetery, a footbridge crosses the busy highway, allowing a clear view of the fabulous **mural (6)** of Kraków history. From here, a switchback trail leads up to the prehistoric pagan ritual site known as **Krakus Mound (7**; p84). From the top of the mound, you can gaze into the **Liban Quarry (8)**,

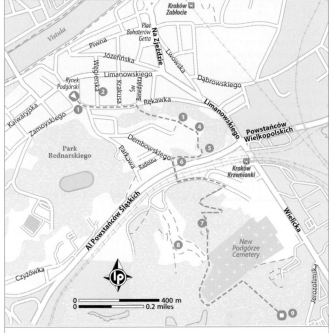

distance 5km **duration** three hours ▶ **start** Rynek Podgórski 🚊 3, 6, 11, 23
● **end** ul Wielicka 🚊 3, 6, 13, 24, 34

an old limestone quarry that has been left for the birds and the bees. Follow the footpath around the edge of the quarry (southwest of the cemetery) and make your way to the unkempt grounds of the former **Płaszów Camp** (9; see the

boxed text, opposite). After paying your respects at the various memorials, you can walk down to ul Wielicka and catch a tram back to the other side of the river.

>WESTERN KRAKÓW

Wander west of the Old Town and you'll discover Kraków at its most artistic and its most verdant. This area was developed at the end of the 19th century, when Kraków was infused with Art Nouveau. Stroll along ul Retoryka and ul Marszał Piłsudskiego for an architectural tour of ornate brickwork, grotesque gargoyles, stained-glass windows and other oddities.

Outside the dual-carriageway ring road, the city morphs into a refreshing green space. The long narrow Błonia Park often hosts concerts, festivals and other mass events, while Jordan's Park to the north was the country's first public playground. Further west is the woodsy suburb of Zwierzyniec, site of two monumental mounds, both of which offer wonderful city views. At the city's edge, the 485-hectare Wolski Forest, or Las Wolski, is a perfect retreat for hikers and bikers, animal-lovers and monks.

WESTERN KRAKÓW

Please see over for map

SEE

JÓZEF MEHOFFER HOUSE

Dom Józefa Mehoffera; ☎ 012 292 6448;
www.muzeum.krakow.pl; ul Krupnicza
26; adult/concession 6/3zł, Sun free;
🕙 10am-6pm Tue-Sat, to 4pm Sun;
🚋 2, 4, 8, 12, 13, 14, 15, 24

The 'Young Poland' artist lived in
this stately home from 1932 until
his death in 1946. The museum
preserves the elegant interiors,
with many original furnishings
and artwork. Look out for work by
the artist, including stained-glass
windows and portraits of his wife.
Be sure not to miss the lovely
garden (p96).

KOŚCIUSZKO MOUND

Kopiec Kościuszki; ☎ 012 425 1116;
www.kopieckosciuszki.pl; al Waszyngto-
na; adult/concession 12/7zł; 🕙 9am-
11pm; 🚌 1, 2, 6 to Salwator; 🚻

The human-made Kościuszko
Mound pays tribute to Tadeusz
Kościuszko, the hero who embod-
ied the dreams of independent
Poland in times of foreign occupation. Enter through the chapel and
climb 34m for a spectacular panorama. There is a separate waxworks
exhibition called Polish Routes to
Independence (adult/child 8/6zł;
open 9.30am to 6.30pm). From Salwator, take bus 100 or walk about
1.5km to the monument.

REMEMBER YOU MUST DIE

Memento Mori is the motto of the Camaldolese monks: remember you must die. Just to make
sure they live by this motto, the monks keep the skulls of their predecessors in their hermit
ages. It is just one of many practices that have earned this ancient order its reputation for
asceticism and austerity. The monks do not sleep in coffins, as rumoured, but they do live in
seclusion, with contact only during prayers. They are vegetarian and eat their meals alone.
Some monks have no contact with the outside world at all.

Part of the Benedictine family of monastic communities, the Camaldolese order came to
Poland from Italy in 1603. Kraków was the first of the Camaldolese seats in Poland; a church
and 20 hermitages were established on Srebrna Góra (Silver Mountain; see p94) between
1603 and 1642, and the whole complex was walled in. Not much has changed since.

A long walled alley leads to the main gate, the ceiling of which is covered in naive fres-
coes. Opposite the entrance is the massive white limestone facade of the monastery church
(50m high and 40m wide). A spacious, single-nave interior is covered by a barrel-shaped
vault and lined on both sides with eight ornate Baroque chapels. Underneath the chancel of
the church is the crypt of the hermits. Bodies are placed into niches without coffins and then
sealed. Latin inscriptions state the age of the deceased and the period spent in the hermitage.
The niches are opened after 80 years and most of the remains moved to a place of permanent
rest. It's then that the hermits take the skulls to keep them company in their shelters.

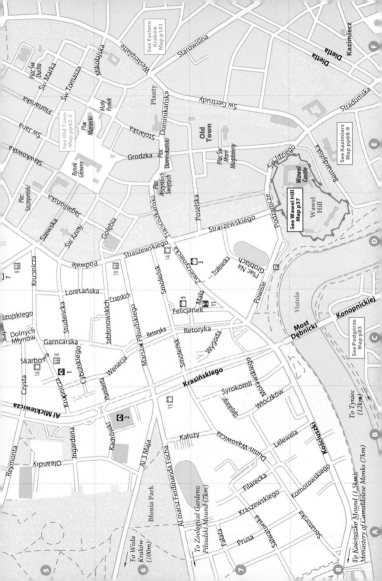

See Eastern Kraków Map p101

Starowiślna

Dietla

Dietla

Kazimierz

Wesoła

Plac Św Ducha

Pl Św Marka

Sw Tomasza

Nikolajska

Mały Rynek

Planty

Św Gertrudy

Stradomska

Florianska

Sw Tomasza

Pl Mariacki

Dominikańska

See Old Town Map pp42-3

Św Jana

Stolarska

Plac Dominikański

See Kazimierz Map pp68-9

Bernardyńska

Sławkowska

Grodzka

Old Town

Pl Św Marii Magdaleny

Św Idziego

Rynek Główny

Pl Szczepański

Jagiellońska

Pl Wszystkich Świętych

Poselska

Wawel Castle

Szewska

Sw Anny

Franciszkańska

Straszewskiego

Podzamcze

See Wawel Hill Map p37

Wawel Hill

Gołębia

Podwale

Straszewskiego

Smoleńsk

Zwierzyniecka

Tarłowska

Plac Na Groblach

Krupnicza

Loretańska

Czapskich

14

3

Powiśle

Vistula

9

7

Szujskiego

Studencka

Jabłonowskich

Marszałka Piłsudskiego

Retoryka

5

Felicjanek

11

Mała

Konopnickiej

Dolnych Młynów

Garncarska

Cybulskiego

Wenecja

Retoryka

Smoleńsk

Wygoda

Most Dębnicki

See Podgórze Map p83

Skarbowa

16

Lambert

Krupnicza

1

8

Krasińskiego

Syrokomli

Morawskiego

To Tyniec (12km)

Czysta

Kadłówki

2

6

15

Włóczków

Lelewela

Kościuszki

Al Michiewicza

Al 3 Maja

Kałuży

Dunin-Wąsowicza

Reymonta

Ingardena

Oleandry

Błonia Park

Almarsz Ferdinanda Focha

Filarecka

Kraszewskiego

Komorowskiego

To Wisła Kraków (100m)

To Zoological Gardens; Piłsudski Mound (7km)

Smoleńska

Falata

Prusa

Salwatorska

Sanatoryjna

To Kościuszko Mound (1.5km); Monastery of Camaldolese Monks (7km)

◎ MONASTERY OF CAMALDOLESE MONKS

Klasztor Kamedułów; ☎ 012 429 7610; www.kameduli.info, in Polish; Srebrna Góra; ⏲ 8-11am & 3-4.30pm; 🚍 1, 6 to Salwator

The mighty Monastery of Ca-maldolese Monks sits atop Silver Mountain, overlooking the Vistula (Wisła) River (see the boxed text, p91). Men can visit the church and crypt any day, but women can enter the complex only on certain feast days (see website for details). From Salwator take any west-bound bus except 100; you can also follow the marked trail 1km south from the zoo.

◎ NATIONAL MUSEUM – MAIN BUILDING

Muzeum Narodowe – Gmach Główny; ☎ 012 295 5500; www.muzeum .krakow.pl; al 3 Maja 1; adult/concession 18/12zł, Sun free; ⏲ 10am-6pm Tue-Sat, to 3pm Sun; 🚍 15, 18; ♿

The so-called Main Building of the National Museum in Kraków hous-es three permanent exhibitions – the Gallery of 20th-Century Polish Painting, the Gallery of Decorative Art, and Polish Arms and National Colours – plus various temporary exhibitions. The excellent painting gallery includes art from 1890 until the present day.

A long way from home: red-necked wallabies at Kraków's Zoological Gardens

◉ PIŁSUDSKI MOUND

Kopiec Piłsudskiego; Las Wolski; admission free; ⏱ 24hr; 🚌 134

Within the confines of Wolski Forest, the 35m Piłsudski Mound is the tallest of the four city mounds. Using soil taken from WWI battle sites, it was erected in honour of the marshal Józef Piłsudski after his death in 1935. The mound is about 1km north of the zoo; otherwise, walkers can follow a well-marked trail from the Kościuszko Mound.

◉ ZOOLOGICAL GARDENS

☎ 012 425 3551; www.zoo-krakow.pl; ul Kasy Oszczędności Miasta Krakowa 14; adult/concession 14/7zł; ⏱ 9am-3pm Nov-Mar, to 5pm Apr, May, Sep & Oct, to 7pm Jun-Aug; 🚌 134; ♿

In the midst of forested Las Wolski, the Kraków zoo hosts more than 260 species, including Indian elephants, pygmy hippos and various rare species of antelope. It is also home to a herd of Przewalski horses, which are no longer found in the wild.

⬛ SHOP

◻ GRIM SALON JUBILERSKI *Jewellery*

☎ 012 421 7128; ul Zwierzyniecka 10; ⏱ 10am-6pm Mon-Sat; 🚋 1, 2, 6

There is nothing grim about this jeweller, which exudes the golden glow of amber. The showroom is jam-packed with jewellery, lamps, dishware and other amber-encrusted treats.

◻ KSIĘGARNIA POD GLOBUSEM *Bookstore*

☎ 012 430 0445; ul Długa 1; ⏱ 10am-7pm Mon-Fri, to 2pm Sat; 🚋 3, 5, 7

This 'bookstore under the globe' carries a great selection of maps and travel guides. Look for the landmark green copper globe perched atop the steeple of the amazing Art Nouveau building.

◻ MASSOLIT BOOKS & CAFÉ *Bookstore*

☎ 012 432 4150; www.massolit.com; ul Felicjanek 4; ⏱ 10am-8pm Sun-Thu, to 9pm Fri & Sat; 🚋 1, 2, 6; ✗

You could spend the entire afternoon browsing your way through the city's best English-language bookstore. This multiroom treasure trove sells new and secondhand fiction and nonfiction, with an excellent selection of Polish history and literature in translation.

◻ STARY KLEPARZ *Market*

☎ 012 634 1532; www.starykleparz .com; ul Paderewskiego; ⏱ 7am-6pm Mon-Sat; 🚋 3, 5, 7

The city's most atmospheric and historic place to shop for fresh fruits, vegetables and flowers is this sprawling covered market, which dates back to the 12th century. You'll also find meats, cheeses, spices and bread, as well as clothes and other necessities.

☐ TRABANT MUSIC BOX
Music
☎ 790 395 564; ul Karmelicka 18/4;
⏱ 9am-6pm Mon-Fri, to 4pm Sat; 🚊 4, 8, 12, 13, 14, 24

It's not only for music, but also coffee and the occasional art exhibit. But music is what Trabant does best, especially local indie-rock and jazz.

🍴 EAT
🍴 CAFE WAŻKA
Polish €
☎ 665 203 542; ul Krupnicza 26;
⏱ 10am-10pm; 🚊 2, 4, 8, 12, 13, 14, 15, 24

A handful of tables are carefully arranged around a leafy oak tree in the blooming garden of the Mehoffer house. (In case of rain, you can sit inside the cosy cafe.) Service is leisurely, so sit back and enjoy the delightful setting.

Art imitating life at hot-pink and happening Różowy Słoń

◨ DYNIA
European €€

☎ 012 430 0838; www.dynia.krakow
.pl; ul Krupnicza 20; ⏱ 8.30am-10pm;
🚃 2, 4, 8, 12, 13, 14, 15, 24; ✗ Ⓥ
While Dynia's interior is chic – with
leather furniture and avant-garde
floral arrangements – it is the gorgeous, green courtyard that is so
enticing. Crumbling brick walls sur-
round the fern-filled space, evok-
ing an atmosphere of elegance
amid decay. The menu is a modern
European mix, with a few low-cal
options on the 'fitness menu'.

◨ MAMMA MIA
Pizzeria €€

☎ 012 430 0492; www.mammamia.net
.pl; ul Karmelicka 14; ⏱ noon-11pm;
🚃 4, 8, 12, 13, 14, 24; ✗ ⓐ Ⓥ ⓑ
We know you didn't come to Poland to eat pizza, but if you have
a craving, go for the delicious,
crispy, thin-crusted pies that come
out of the wood-burning oven at
Mamma Mia.

◨ RÓŻOWY SŁOŃ
Cafeteria €

☎ 012 421 1047; ul Straszewskiego
24; ⏱ 9am-8pm Mon-Sat, 11am-7pm
Sun; 🚃 2, 7, 8, 15; ✗ ⓑ
Pepto-pink plastic furniture and
mural-painted walls liven up the
milk-bar atmosphere at the 'pink
elephant'. So this is what they
mean when they say 'See you in

the funny papers'. Recommended
for *naleśniki* (crêpes).

DRINK
☿ CAFÉ SZAFE *Cafe*

☎ 601 877 993; www.cafeszafe.com; ul
Felicjanek 10; ⏱ 9am-1am Mon-Fri, 10am-
midnight Sat & Sun; 🚃 1, 2, 6; 🛜 ⓑ
The colourful cafe on the corner
is a cupboard full of surprises,
from the whimsical sculptured
creatures lurking in the corners to
the intriguing artwork that hangs
on the walls. The place hosts concerts, films and other arty events.

PLAY
☆ CIEMNIA CLUB *Gay Club*

☎ 069 265 1311; www.ciemnia.com.pl;
ul Krowoderska 8; ⏱ 7pm-2am Sun-Thu,
to 5am Fri & Sat; 🚃 3, 5, 7
Ciemnia translates as 'darkroom'.
This is Kraków's premier gay bar,
with facilities intended for those
seriously OFB (out for business).
There is a strictly enforced dress
code, which involves leaving some
(or all) of your clothing in the
cloakroom. Men only.

☆ EL SOL *Latin Club*

☎ 012 633 8835; www.elsol-krakow.pl;
ul Batorego 1; ⏱ 7pm-midnight Sun-
Thu, to 3am Fri & Sat; 🚃 4, 8, 12, 13,
14, 24
This Latino club reverberates to
the sound of salsa, merengue,

DETOUR: TYNIEC

A distant suburb of Kraków, 12km southwest of the centre, Tyniec is the site of the **Benedictine Abbey of SS Peter & Paul** (Opactwo Benedyktynów; ☎ 012 688 5200; www.tyniec.benedyktyni.pl; ul Benedyktyńska 37), dramatically perched on a cliff above the Vistula River. You enter the complex through a pair of defensive gates, resembling the entrance to a castle, and find yourself in a large courtyard. To the southwest is an octagonal wooden pavilion, which protects a stone well dating from 1620. In the building further west, you can see the foundations of earlier churches that stood on this site. Most importantly, the on-site store sells cheese, honey, beer and other Benedictine goodies.

Spiritual seekers can make arrangements to spend a day in prayer and meditation. Otherwise, the church is open to all for regularly scheduled Masses or for a look around. Behind a sober facade, the dark interior is fitted out with a mix of Baroque and Rococo furnishings; up to the left are the remnants of early wall paintings. The organ is plain but has a beautiful tone, and concerts are held here in summer. Have a look at the exuberant Rococo pulpit.

To reach the abbey, take bus 112 from the Rondo Grunwaldzkie, the roundabout on the west side of Grunwald Bridge. Alternatively, rent a bike and ride west along the path that follows the south bank of the river.

samba and bossa nova. Tuesday night is salsa night (with lessons), while Thursdays cater especially to the Columbian community.

⭐ FILHARMONIA KRAKOWSKA
Classical Music

Kraków Philharmonic; ☎ 012 422 4312; www.filharmonia.krakow.pl; ul Zwierzyniecka 1; tickets 18-40zł; ⏲ box office noon-7pm Tue-Fri, 1hr before performance Sat & Sun; 🚊 2, 7, 8, 15
This Baroque building on the southwest edge of the Planty is home to one of the country's best symphony orchestras, as well as a large mixed choir, a boys' choir and several small ensembles.

⭐ SCENA STU *Theatre*
☎ 012 422 2744; www.scenastu.com.pl, in Polish; Aleja Krasińskiego 16/18; ⏲ box office 9am-7pm Mon-Fri, 2hr before performance Sat & Sun; 🚊 1, 2, 6
The 'STU Stage' started in the 1970s as a politically involved student theatre and was immediately successful. Today it is a solid professional troupe performing avant-garde plays.

⭐ TEATR GROTESKA *Theatre*
☎ 012 633 3762; www.groteska.pl; ul Skarbowa 2; ⏲ box office 8am-noon & 3-5pm Mon-Fri & 1hr before performance; 🚊 2, 4, 8, 12, 13, 14, 15, 24; 🚹
The 'Grotesque Theatre' stages puppet and mask shows for adults

and children. The theatre is especially known for its creepy, word-
less version of *The Golem*, the story
of a Frankenstein-like clay creature
brought to life by a Prague rabbi.
Also hosts the Grand Dragon
Parade (p25) in early June.

⭐ WISŁA KRAKÓW
Spectator Sport
☎ 012 630 7600; www.wisla.krakow.pl;
ul Reymonta 22; 🚋 15, 18
Poland's most successful football
club, Wisła Kraków has won seven
Polish championships in the past
decade. It is particularly strong
in its home stadium, which is a
back-up venue for the Euro 2012
tournament.

Welome to the 'Grotesque Theatre'

>EASTERN KRAKÓW

Kraków Głowny train station is the first port of call for most visitors to Kraków. From here, they beat a hasty retreat into the Old Town, only to emerge several days later to board their train out of town.

Many never experience Kraków outside the Planty, yet here the city pulses to a different beat. Poles bustle to and from their homes and jobs; they ride trams and go shopping and live their lives. Here, Kraków loses its aura of medieval magic and holiday haven, and takes on the rhythms of the workaday world.

You are unlikely to spend too much time wandering the streets east of the Old Town, but you might be enticed by the blooms in the botanical gardens or the isolation of the Jewish Cemetery. The city's dramatic new opera theatre lures culture vultures for a night out, while parents will appreciate the excellent array of rainy-day activities. And in the far eastern reaches, the suburb of Nowa Huta recalls the city's not-too-distant communist-era past.

EASTERN KRAKÓW

🅞 SEE
Botanical Gardens **1** C4
Kraków Aquarium **2** A5
New Jewish Cemetery ...**3** B6
St Florian's Church **4** A3

🅞 SHOP
Galeria Krakowska **5** B3
Hala Targowa **6** B5

🍴 EAT
Bar Wegatariański
   VEGA **7** A5
Klimaty Południa **8** A5

⭐ PLAY
Kitsch ....(see 9)
Łubu-Dubu **9** A5
Opera Krakowska **10** C3

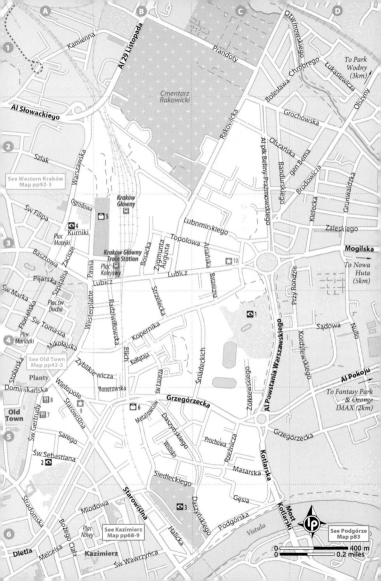

Map Labels

Grid references and streets:

Kamienna
Prandoty
Al 29 Listopada
Otwinowskiego
Bolesława Chrobrego
Łukasiewicza
To Park Wodny (3km)
Cmentarz Rakowicki
Al Słowackiego
Rakowicka
Olszary
Grochowska
Olszańska
Szlak
Warszawska
Al płk Beliny-Prażmowskiego
gen Bema
Bandurskiego
Grochowska
Gruniwaldzka
See Western Kraków Map pp92-3
Ogrodowa
Kraków Główny
Lubomirskiego
Kielecka
Zaleskiego
Mogilska
Św Filipa
Kurniki
Plac Matejki
Topolowa
Ariańska
To Nowa Huta (5km)
Basztowa
Zacisze
Szpitalna
Pawia
Kraków Główny Train Station
Bosacka
Zygmunta Augusta
Plac Kolejowy
Lubicz
Botaniczna
Przy Rondzie
Pijarska
Westerplatte
Radziwiłłowska
Strzelecka
Sądowa
Św Marka
Florańska
Św Ducha
Plac św Ducha
Kopernika
Nulto
Św Tomasza
Mikołajska
Blich
Kołłątaja
Śniadeckich
Al Powstania Warszawskiego
Kordylewskiego
Plac Mariacki
Żyblikiewicza
Św Łazarza
Żółkiewskiego
Al Pokoju
See Old Town Map pp42-3
Wielopole
Planty
Dominikańska
Ronerowska
Grzegórzecka
To Fantasy Park & Orange IMAX (2km)
Old Town
Starowiślna
Metalowców
Grzegórzecka
Stolarska
Św Gertrudy
Daszyńskiego
Wielicko
Prochowa
Rzeźnicza
Kotlarska
Sarego
Reformacka
Masarska
Św Sebastiana
Stradomska
Daszyńskiego
Gęsia
Most Kotlarski
Podgórska
Miodowa
Bożego Ciała
Plac Nowy
Siedleckiego
See Kazimierz Map pp68-9
Halicka
Vistula
See Podgórze Map p83
Dietla
Meiselsa
Kazimierz
Św Wawrzyńca

0   400 m
0   0.2 miles

👁 SEE

👁 BOTANICAL GARDENS

Ogród Botaniczny; ☎ **012 421 2620;
www.ogrod.uj.edu.pl; ul Kopernika 27;
admission 5zł;** 🕑 **garden 9am-7pm
daily, greenhouses 10am-6pm Sat-Thu,
museum 10am-2pm Wed & Fri, 11am-
3pm Sat;** 🚃 **4, 5, 9, 10, 15, 40;** ♿

The botanical gardens of Jagiellonian University are nearly 10
hectares of green and flowery
loveliness. Besides the fresh air
and beautiful blooms, the gardens
offer fascinating exhibits of medic-
inal plants, endangered species of
Polish flora and plants described
in the Bible. The amazing orchid
collection dates to the 1860s.

👁 KRAKÓW AQUARIUM

☎ **012 429 1049; www.aquarium
krakow.com; ul Św Sebastiana 9;
adult/concession 18/12zł;** 🕑 **9am-8pm
Mon-Fri, to 9pm Sat & Sun;** 🚃 **3, 6, 8, 10,
18, 19, 40;** ♿

Your kids will love the chance to get
up close and personal with dozens
of fish, turtles, snakes and lizards.
The smallish facility packs more
than 130 species into its urban location, with aquatic creatures on the
ground floor and reptiles (plus a set
of furry marmosets!) upstairs.

👁 NEW JEWISH CEMETERY

**Nowy Cmentarz Żidowsky; ul Miodowa
55;** 🕑 **8am-6pm Sun-Fri;** 🚃 **9, 34**

Although it's the 'new' Jewish cemetery, it was established as early as
1800. There are some 9000 surviving tombstones, some of which
have eerie and elaborate carvings.

👁 ST FLORIAN'S CHURCH

Kościół Św Floriana; ☎ **012 422 4842;
ul Warszawska 1b;** 🚃 **2, 4, 5, 7, 12, 13,
14, 15, 24**

This 12th-century church's location
was apparently chosen by the oxen
that carried the holy relics of St Florian from Rome. When the beasts
of burden would go no further, it
was taken as a sign of a holy site.
In 1582, the church survived a fire
that swept through the city; since
then, St Florian has been considered a patron saint of Kraków
and of firefighters. The nearby
monument celebrates the 1410
Battle of Grunwald, when the Poles
defeated the Teutonic Knights.

🛍 SHOP

🛍 GALERIA KRAKOWSKA
Shopping Mall

www.galeria-krakowska.pl; 🕑 **9am-
10pm Mon-Sat, 10am-9pm Sun;** 🚃 **7, 10,
18, 19, 24, 34, 40;** ♿

In case there was any question
about Poland transitioning to
capitalism, here's your answer. The
massive mall near the train station
contains 270 stores; of interest to
world-weary travellers are the food
court and American bookstore.

Majestic tombstones at Kraków's 'new' Jewish Cemetery

HALA TARGOWA *Market*
Ul Grzegórzecka 3; ⏰ **7am-3pm;** 🚋 **1, 7, 9, 11, 22;**

This outdoor flea market is pretty much the opposite of the Galeria Krakowska. You'll find lots of old books with yellowed pages, postcards depicting the Kraków of yesteryear, paintings and icons, and loads of other trash and treasure. Vendors set up here daily but Sunday before noon is best.

🍴 EAT

🍴 BAR WEGETARIAŃSKI VEGA
Vegetarian   €

☎ **012 422 3494; www.vegarestauracja .com.pl; ul Św Gertrudy 7;** ⏰ **9am-9pm;** 🚋 **7, 10, 13, 19, 24, 34, 40;** ❌ Ⓥ

Although there's no table service, this vegetarian restaurant pulls off a romantic atmosphere, with candle lighting and lace table-cloths. The impressively varied menu includes such things as soy and oat cutlets, pancakes, dumplings, casseroles and breakfasts, as well as a lengthy list of teas.

🍴 KLIMATY POŁUDNIA
European   €€

☎ **012 422 0357; www.klimatypoludnia .pl; ul Św Gertrudy 5;** ⏰ **1pm-midnight;** 🚋 **7, 10, 13, 19, 24, 34, 40**

Wander away from the busy street, through the courtyard, to this hidden gem. The menu is vaguely Mediterranean, though Polish and other influences are evident. A good wine list and cosy quarters make it an excellent stop.

⭐ PLAY

⭐ FANTASY PARK
Bowling & Billiards

☎ 012 290 9515; www.fantasypark.pl; al Pokoju 44, Kraków Plaza; bowling per hr 54-94zł, kids per hr 10-15zł; 🕙 10am-2am; 🚊 1, 14, 22; ♿

There's something for everyone at the high-energy Fantasy Park. The main attraction is the 20 tenpin bowling lanes, but you can also entertain yourself with billiards, video games or good old-fashioned drinking at the bar. There's a supervised play area for the little ones.

⭐ KITSCH *Nightclub*

☎ 012 422 5299; www.kitsch.pl; 4th fl, ul Wielopole 15; 🕙 7pm-last guest; 🚊 1, 7, 9, 11, 22

Poles seem to think that this is a gay club. Certainly it's a queer-friendly place, but people of all persuasions find their way to Kitsch for a night of drunken dancing and shameless mashing.

⭐ ŁUBU-DUBU *Nightclub*

☎ 694 461 402; www.lubu-dubu.pl; 2nd fl, ul Wielopole 15; 🕙 4pm-4am; 🚊 1, 7, 9, 11, 22

Feeling nostalgic for the bad old days? Get your fix at this retro bar that hearkens back to the days of communism and Kool & the Gang. Never mind that most of the patrons are too young to remember the 1980s…

⭐ OPERA KRAKOWSKA *Opera*

☎ 012 296 6100; www.opera.krakow.pl; ul Lubicz 48; tickets 40-80zł; 🕙 box office 10am-7pm Mon-Fri; 🚊 1, 4, 5, 9, 10; ♿

The Kraków Opera performs in the striking, modern, red building at the Mogilskie roundabout – brand new in 2009. The setting is decidedly 21st century, but the repertoire spans the ages, incorporating everything from Verdi to Bernstein.

⭐ ORANGE IMAX *Cinema*

☎ 012 290 9080; www.kinoimax.pl, in Polish; al Pokoju 44, Kraków Plaza; adult/concession 21/18zł; 🚊 1, 14, 22; ♿

The great thing about IMAX theatres is that you don't need to understand the words to appreciate the incredible cinematography surrounding you. Some of the nature films are 3D, which means you might actually feel that snapping turtle nip you on the nose.

⭐ PARK WODNY *Water Park*

☎ 012 616 3190; www.parkwodny.pl; ul Dobrego Pasterza 126; 2hr admission adult/concession Mon-Fri 29/24zł, Sat & Sun 31/27zł; 🕙 8am-10pm; 🚊 129, 152; ♿

Your skin will be wrinkled and prunelike by the time you leave this fun-filled aqua park, located 2.5km northeast of the Old Town. For endless hours of wet and wild, there are paddling pools, water sports, 800m of water slides, saltwater hot tubs, saunas and more.

Agnieszka Perek
Curator at the Nowa Huta Museum, wizard of sociology and city planning, Nowa Huta born and bred

What makes Nowa Huta unique in Kraków? Nowa Huta was built as a 'garden city' so that grand buildings would be interspersed with nature and greenery. **When to visit** It's lovely in spring and autumn, while summer is an exciting time for outside exhibitions. **Best cultural event** Nowa Huta Film Festival (www.nhfestiwal.pl, in Polish) in August. **Exciting developments in Nowa Huta** Łaźnia Nowa (p108) does amazing, experimental theatre that involves members of the community and tells their stories. **Where do you go on your day off?** Nowa Huta Meadows (p108). It's just a few blocks away, but you feel you have escaped the city. On a clear day you can see the Tatra Mountains.

Worth the Trip: Nowa Huta

A special gift from 'Uncle Joe' Stalin to the Polish people, the suburb of Nowa Huta was built in 1949. The 'New Steelworks' consisted of a massive factory and a modern residential area to house the workforce. This carefully planned community was a socialist experiment that attracted thousands of workers who brought their families to create a new society.

Needless to say, the experiment went awry. For starters, residents resisted the idea that their utopia should have no church. Later, the steelworkers were a stronghold in the Solidarity labour movement. And the suburb is still dealing with the factory's devastating environmental impact.

Despite this chequered, proletarian past, residents have a right to be proud of the suburb's revolutionary role – both as socialist experiment and as instrument of change. Never straying from these roots, Nowa Huta now hosts an intriguing cultural movement, enticing visionaries as a sort of up-and-coming, post-industrial artistic destination.

See

The main thoroughfare is **Aleja Róż** (Alley of the Roses), a grand promenade that terminates at the main central square, surrounded by neoclassical architecture. A statue of Vladimir Ilych Lenin once stood here. Locals love to tell about the bomb that exploded here in 1979, revealing some residents' true feelings about the Soviet leader, but the explosion actually did little damage. That statue was removed in 1989, and Plac Centralny is now officially named after Ronald Reagan.

Two blocks north of Plac Centralny, the **Nowa Huta Museum** (☎ 012 425 9775; www.mhk.pl; os Słoneczne; adult/concession 5/3zł, Tue free; 🕙 9.30am-5pm Tue-Sat May-Oct, 9am-4pm Tue-Sat Nov-Apr; 🚊 4, 14, 15) is more like a glorified tourist office, but there is a small, well-curated exhibit space. Rotating exhibits incorporate multimedia to explore the neighbourhood's controversial history and contemporary development.

The beloved **Arka Pana** (Lord's Ark; ☎ 012 644 0624; www.arkapana.pl, in Polish; ul Obrońców Krzyża; 🚊 14) was the first church in Nowa Huta, built in 1977 after much controversy. Authorities had intended the suburb to be a church-free zone, and it required protests and politicking by the local bishop (one Karol Wojtyła, who would later become pope) to get the job done. Across the street, a small **monument** marks the spot where a steelworker was killed while protesting communist rule.

You can't actually go inside the massive **steelworks complex** (ul Ujastek 1; 🚊 4) at the east end of the suburb, but it's worth riding the tram to the entrance, which is marked with a huge sign for Huta im Tadeusza Sendzimira (pictured pp106-7). (Originally named after Lenin, the factory adopted the name of this Polish-American inventor in 1989.) The castlelike administrative buildings reflect the Renaissance style that was declared to be Poland's 'national form'.

Want to see Nowa Huta in proletarian style? **Crazy Guides** (☎ 012 421 1327; www .crazyguides.com; ul Floriańska 44; tour 119-169zł) will drive you around in a vintage Trabant, the East German 'car of the people'. The 'deluxe' version of the tour includes a driving lesson and a visit with a real live communist.

Eat
If you thought you backtracked about 20 years when you arrived in Nowa Huta, the 'stylish' **Restauracja Stylowa** (☎ 012 644 2619; os Centrum C3; 🕙 9am-11pm; 🚊 4, 14, 15) will confirm it. This local legend on the central square was the suburb's most elegant eatery, and it probably still is. Ladies with variously coloured hair will bring you delicious soups and filling *pierogi* (dumplings) for pennies.

Drink
Nowa Huta has come a long way since 1949, when the steelworks and suburb were built. Opposite the museum, the funky **Club 1949** (☎ 012 565 9190; www.1949club.pl; os Urocze 12; 🕙 9am-9pm; 🚊 4, 14, 15; 🛜) pays tribute to the 'hood, with local street signs and propaganda posters adorning the walls.

Inside the Łaźnia Nowa building, the eclectic **Klub Kombinator** (☎ 012 425 0320; os Szkolne 25; 🕙 11am-late; 🚊 4, 14, 15; 🛜) attracts creative types who hang out, smoke, drink vodka and play cards. On weekends, the place is packed with artsy-looking people, especially before or after a show.

Play
It's worth a visit to the **Teatr Ludowy** (People's Theatre; ☎ 012 680 2112; www.ludowy.pl; os Teatralna 34; 🚊 4, 14, 15) just to admire the proletarian architecture. Built in 1955, the theatre was known for its experimental, avant-garde productions. Equally innovative, the **Łaźnia Nowa** (☎ 012 425 0320; www.laznianowa.pl; os Szkolne 25; 🚊 4, 14, 15) has converted an old workshop into an experimental art space, with two stages and plenty of creative juice.

When you want to escape, retreat to **Nowa Huta Meadows** (Novohuckie Łąki), where walking trails wind through overgrown meadows, with a small section of manicured gardens.

>EXCURSIONS

Serene sculpture of Copernicus hewn entirely from salt, Wieliczka Salt Mine (p113)

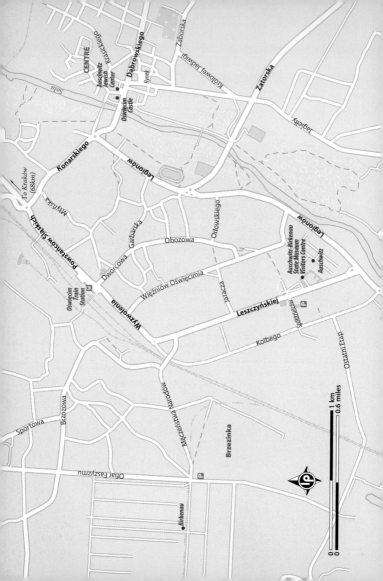

AUSCHWITZ-BIRKENAU

In 1940, on the outskirts of the small town of Oświęcim, the Nazis established a concentration camp that was to become the largest experiment in genocide in the history of humankind. Most commonly known by its German name, Auschwitz originally held Polish political prisoners. It was later designated for the extermination of Jews, and a much larger facility was constructed at nearby Birkenau. It has been estimated that around 1.5 million people, including 1.1 million Jews, were systematically murdered here.

Today both camps have been preserved as the **Auschwitz-Birkenau State Museum.** You can tour the grounds yourself using the useful *Auschwitz-Birkenau Guidebook* (5zł) or join a guided tour in the language of your choice (39zł).

The smaller Auschwitz camp was only partially destroyed by the fleeing Nazis, and many of the buildings remain. Start your visit by watching the 17-minute **documentary film** (adult/concession 3.50/2.50zł), screened in the visitor centre, about the 1945 liberation of the camp by Soviet troops. Then proceed through the infamous gates bearing the slogan 'Arbeit Macht Frei' (Work Sets You Free).

The barracks hold separate exhibitions dedicated to the creation of the camp, confiscation of personal property, daily life and labour, and the resistance movement. While many of the exhibits are intended to shock, to try to express the scope of the tragedy that took place here, none is more horrifying than the massive sea of human hair (found in **Block 4**) that was collected and sold to make cloth.

INFORMATION
Location Oświęcim, 40km west of Kraków
Getting there Frequent buses (8zł, 90 minutes) travel to Oświęcim, dropping passengers in the parking lot of the Auschwitz-Birkenau State Museum. Hourly trains (11zł, 90 minutes) go to the Oświęcim train station, from where you can catch a local bus (24, 25, 28 or 29) or a taxi (15zł).
Contact Auschwitz-Birkenau State Museum (Państwowe Muzeum Auschwitz-Birkenau; ☎ 033 843 2022; www.auschwitz.org.pl; ul Więźniów Oświęcimia 20; admission by donation; ☼ 8am-7pm Jun-Aug, to 6pm May & Sep, to 5pm Apr & Oct, to 4pm Mar & Nov, to 3pm Dec-Feb)

The chilling remains of Auschwitz-Birkenau State Museum

Block 11 is the notorious 'Death Block'. In the courtyard, thousands of victims were lined up and shot in front of the Wall of Death. The basement contains cells where prisoners were tortured, held in solitary confinement and starved to death.

Other blocks focus on the various nationalities that died here; the most informative is the excellent exhibit about the Roma people. At one end of the grounds, you can actually enter the **gas chamber** and **crematoria**.

Most mass killings actually took place at the vast **Birkenau** camp, also known as Auschwitz II, which is about 2km to the west. Although much of the camp was destroyed by the retreating Nazis, visiting Birkenau is an essential part of the memorial experience. Catch the free shuttle bus that runs between the two camps.

Train tracks run right through the centre of the Birkenau grounds. Here the selection process took place: some passengers were sent to labour as slaves and live in the squalor of the barracks (some of which still stand and are open for viewing); other passengers were herded off the train and sent directly to the gas chambers (which have been left in ruins). The sheer size of this place gives some idea of the scope of the crime; climb the tower at the entrance gate to get the full effect.

WIELICZKA SALT MINE

'More than salt', boasts the advert promoting a visit to this ultradeep mine on Kraków's outskirts. But actually, it's nothing more than salt. And that's exactly why it's so impressive. It's an eerie underground world of pits and chambers, filled with finely crafted sculptures and bas reliefs, and *everything* has been carved by hand from salt.

The mine has been recognised as a Unesco World Heritage site for more than 30 years. Even more impressive, the mine has been in operation for 700-plus years.

Tours start with a giddying descent down 380 wooden stairs that reach a depth of 135m. You are taken through a series of chambers, hewn out of the grey-green salt, many with carvings made by miners. They even carved out chapels, including the awesome **Chapel of the Blessed Kinga**. Measuring 54m by 17m, this would be a fair-sized church even if it wasn't hewn completely from salt. There's also an underground lake in the **Eram Barącz Chamber**, and an impressive panoramic viewing platform in the 36m-high **Stanisław Staszic Chamber**.

The tour ends at the **Kraków Saltworks Museum**, accommodated in 14 chambers on level three, but most visitors seem to be over-salted by then. From here a fast mining lift takes you back up to the real world.

The guided tours take two hours and cover about 3km. The temperature in the mine is a steady 15°C, so bring a sweater. English-language tours depart throughout the day (every half-hour in July and August, otherwise every 90 minutes or so).

Your hotel may be able to arrange advance purchase of tickets, which is highly recommended to avoid the long queues at Wieliczka. Otherwise, it is possible to book a tour through one of the agencies in Kraków (p147) for about 110zł per person including transport.

INFORMATION
Location 14km southeast of Kraków city centre, just outside the administrative boundaries
Getting there Frequent minibuses (2.50zł) to Wieliczka depart from Kraków Główny and drop passengers off near the salt mine entrance. Trains between Kraków and Wieliczka (4zł, 25 minutes) leave throughout the day, but the train station in Wieliczka is over 1km from the mine.
Contact Wieliczka Salt Mine (Kopalnia Soli; ☎ 012 278 7302; www.kopalnia.pl; ul Daniłowicza 10; adult/concession/family 64/49/177zł; ☼ 7.30am-7.30pm Apr-Oct, 8am-5pm Nov-Mar)

>SNAPSHOTS

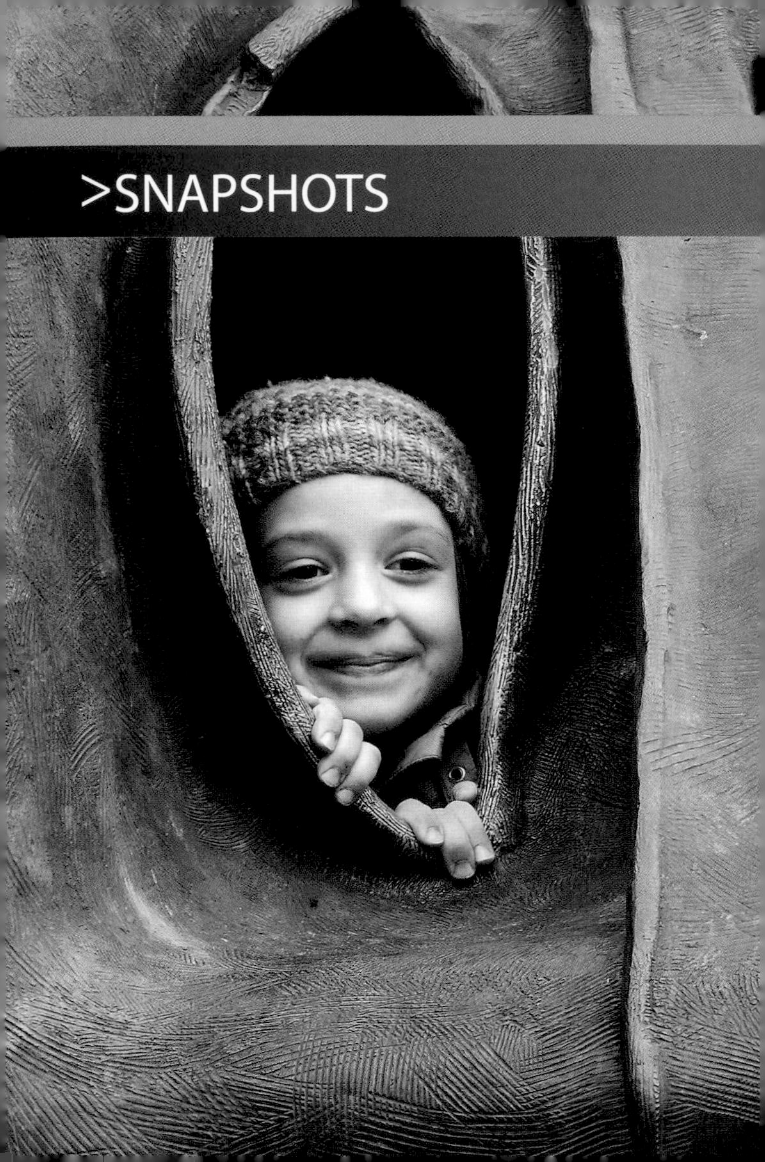

Peek inside Kraków's many sub-cultures to see what's there for you. Eating, drinking, shopping and sleeping are obligatory, but that's only the beginning. Listen to music, pore over a painting, pay your respects to those who have gone before...and always take time to stop and admire the view.

Plenty for kids to enjoy (p126): sculpture by Igor Mitoraj in the Old Town's Rynek Główny

ACCOMMODATION

Kraków is Poland's top tourist destination, so there's no shortage of places to stay. Prices do tend to be above the Polish average, and advance bookings are advisable during the busy Easter, summer and Christmas seasons. Keep in mind that prices will be higher at these times.

The Old Town (Stare Miasto) is the main place to find deluxe and top-end hotels, as well as several excellent, long-enduring midrange establishments. If you have a hankering to stay in a Gothic burgher mansion, or a Renaissance merchant town house, or an Art Nouveau extravaganza, the Old Town is for you. Do note, however, that the Old Town is the centre of the tourist action. Late-opening bars and clubs mean that noise can be a problem if you have a room overlooking busy pedestrian streets.

Kazimierz is a quieter option, offering a more residential setting. With the exception of ul Szeroka, Kazimierz feels more like the 'real Kraków' where Poles actually live. The hotels tend to be smaller and more moderately priced than in the Old Town. Many hotels in Kazimierz aim to recreate the ambience of the former Jewish quarter, with thematic artwork and restaurants, and in one case, a *mikvah* (traditional Jewish bath).

There are many hotels just outside the Planty. They may not be contained within the city walls, but they generally offer the same advantages as the Old Town properties – easy access to the major attractions and impressive historic digs.

Prices do not vary greatly depending on location. The simpler midrange options offer rooms for €50 to €150, while more luxurious rooms are available for €150 and up.

Real budget accommodation is mainly the preserve of hostels. Recent years have seen a proliferation of smart new hostels opening in the Old Town and in Kazimierz. Expect to pay from €10 to €15 for a dorm bed, depending on the size of the room. It's wise to book in advance, as the most popular options do fill up, especially in summer.

Another recent trend is to rent a self-contained apartment, which is ideal if you are travelling in a group or if you intend staying for more than a few days. Rates are usually very reasonable, running from €60 to €100 per night for an apartment sleeping up to four people.

WEB RESOURCES

www.cracow-life.com Offers apartment accommodation plus reviews of hotels and hostels.
www.inyourpocket.com Properties are reviewed by local writers and by past customers. Excellent resource.
www.krakow-tourism.com The official hotel booking service of the city of Kraków.
www.staypoland.com Hotel descriptions, reader comments and booking service for over 100 hotels.
www.travelpoland.pl Includes a comprehensive list of hotels and hostels in the city.

BEST HOSTELRY
> Greg & Tom Hostel (www.gregtom hostel.com)
> Hostel Giraffe (www.hostelgiraffe.pl)
> Hostel Flamingo (www.flamingo -hostel.com)
> Nathan's Villa (www.nathansvilla.com)
> Secret Garden (www.thesecretgarden.pl)

BEST HISTORY
> Alef (www.alef.pl)
> Grand Hotel (www.grand.pl)
> Hotel Saski (www.hotelsaski.com.pl)
> Hotel Pod Różą (www.hotel.com.pl)
> Trecius Guesthouse (www.trecius .krakow.pl)

BEST LUXURY
> Hotel Amadeus (www.hotel -amadeus.pl)
> Hotel Copernicus (www.hotel.com.pl)
> Hotel Pugetów (www.donimirski.com)
> Hotel Stary (www.hotel.com.pl)
> Ostoya Palace (www.ostoyapalace.pl)

BEST LOCATION
> Cracow Hostel (www.cracowhostel.com)
> Dom Polonia (www.wspolnota-polska .krakow.pl)
> Wentzl (www.wentzl.pl)
> Anytime Hostel (www.anytime.com.pl)

EAT

'Eat, drink and loosen your belt.' So goes a favourite Polish aphorism, which should give some indication of how Polish food works. The cuisine is rich in meat and game, thick soups and sauces, and starchy sides such as potatoes and *pierogi*. Are you full yet?

You can't say you've eaten Polish food until you've had many plates of *pierogi*, the crescent-shaped dumplings that are stuffed with cheese, minced meat or sauerkraut. You might want to try *gołąbki* (cabbage leaves stuffed with beef and rice), but don't confuse them with *golonka* (boiled pig's knuckle). If there is one dish that is more Polish than any other, it's *bigos*. Sauerkraut, fresh cabbage, mushrooms and meat (usually pork, game, sausage and/or bacon) cook together over a low flame – the longer the better. The result is a sort of a stew that is rich, tangy and filling.

By Polish standards, Kraków is a food paradise. The Old Town is tightly packed with gastronomic venues catering for every pocket. Many are housed in vaulted cellars or quiet courtyards, offering a romantic, historic atmosphere for your meal. Aside from the wide range of Polish establishments, there is a startling number of Italian restaurants, as well as Chinese, French, Hungarian, Indian, Japanese, Mexican and more.

In recent years, Kazimierz has emerged as a culinary hot spot, with loads of restaurants on ul Szeroka, Plac Nowy and the surrounding streets. Some of these – especially on ul Szeroka – serve the Polish version of Jewish cuisine (with varying degrees of authenticity), but you'll also find pizza and pasta, bagels and burritos. The quintessential Kazimierz food is the *zapiekanka* (see the boxed text, p76).

Indeed, each and every neighbourhood has something special to offer a hungry traveller – even Nowa Huta, where you can dine in the city's most stylish, Soviet-style throwback (see the boxed text, p106).

There is no shortage of fine dining, but budget travellers will also be delighted by their options. Kraków has plenty of low-cost eateries called *bar mleczny* (milk bar) or *jadłodajnia* (like 'diner'). They offer affordable and filling Polish food, often served cafeteria-style so you know exactly what you're getting. See the boxed text, p59, for some recommendations.

BEST FOR POLISH
> Chimera Restaurant (p56)
> Miód Malina (p57)
> Pod Aniołami (p57)
> Polskie Smaki (see boxed text, p59)
> Pierożki U Vincenta (p76)

BEST BREAK FROM POLISH
> Aqua e Vino (p55)
> Cyrano de Bergerac (p56)
> La Campana Trattoria (p57)
> Warsztat (p77)

BEST FOR BREAKFAST
> Bagel Mama (p75)
> Café Camelot (p60)
> Dynia (p97)
> Pod Lwem (p87)
> Polskie Smaki (see boxed text, p59)

BEST FOR VEGETARIANS
> Bar Wegetariański Vega (p103)
> Młynek Café (p76)
> Momo Bar (p76)
> Green Way (p57)

Top left Pleased patrons partaking of *pierogi* **Above** Romantic Café Camelot (p60), perfect for a date or dessert

DRINK

The saddest thing in the world is two people and just one bottle. So say the Poles, who like to drink their vodka *do dna*, or 'to the bottom'. The national drink, vodka *(wódka)* is normally drunk as a shot, followed by a pickle.

Clear vodka is not the only species of the spirit. Indeed, there is a whole spectrum of varieties of vodka, from very sweet to extra dry. These include fruit-flavoured delights, pepper vodka, and the famous *żubrówka*, or 'bison vodka'. The latter is so called because it is flavoured with the grass that bison eat in the Białowieża Forest. If you want to bring home a souvenir, any alcohol store will carry *żubrówka*; or visit Szambelan (p55) to sample some other flavoured vodkas.

These days, Polish drinking habits are changing, with tastes turning to beer instead of (or in addition to) vodka. There are several brands of delicious locally brewed Polish *piwo*, such as Żywiec, Tyskie, Okocim and Lech. Poland does not have a tradition of drinking wine, but that too is changing. Oenophiles will find a few wine bars in Kraków serving a nice selection of imported vintages, including Cava (p87) in Podgórze and Vinoteka La Bodega (p61) in the Old Town.

The Kraków drinking scene is dominated by two types of venue: creative cafes that also serve alcohol, and bohemian bars that also serve coffee. Yes, sometimes it's hard to tell the difference. Kraków seems to specialise in places with an artsy atmosphere, usually furnished with mismatched chairs and tables, eclectic artwork and artefacts, and casu-ally cool-looking patrons. Not too posh but not too pleb, these places welcome all (but not overenthusiastically).

Within this framework, there is an endless array of drinking estab-lishments. Some are basement bars, while others are courtyard cafes. Some have quirky themes, while others are a hotchpotch. Some have art exhibits, while others have reading materials and board games. Some go for old-world charm, while others exude contemporary hip. There's something for everybody, really. Once you find your spot, all you have to do is decide if you're going for the *kawa* (coffee) or the *piwo*.

BEST BASEMENT BARS & COURTYARD CAFES
> Black Gallery (p59)
> Café Bunkier (p60)
> Klub Re (p62)
> Zbliżenia (p78)
> Klubokawiarnia Mleczarnia (p78)

BEST QUIRKY THEMES
> Drukarnia (p87)
> Café Philo (p60)
> Propaganda (p78)
> Singer Café (p78)
> Tram Bar (p61)

Top left A quiet corner for a *kawa* and a read **Above** Propaganda (p78), chock-a-block with communist nostalgia

MUSIC

As home to the world-class Academy of Music, it's no surprise that Kraków is at the forefront of the music scene in Poland. The city's most pre-eminent musical institution is the Filharmonia Krakowska (p98); it's officially the Filharmonia im Karola Szymanowskiega w Krakowie, named for the celebrated composer Karol Szymanowski. Recently celebrating the 100-year anniversary of its founding, the symphony orchestra has hosted an impressive list of guest directors and soloists, often offering concerts in the city's historic digs.

While the Opera Krakowska (p104) has been around since 1954, it was only in 2009 that the company moved into its own theatre – the stunning new opera house on ul Lubicz. In addition to a full repertoire throughout the year, Opera Krakowska hosts a summertime festival with performances at Wawel Castle.

Indeed, there is no shortage of festivals celebrating different kinds of music, including sailors' music (p24), sacred music (p24), ethnic music (p25) and Polish music (p26). One of the most exciting and innovative festivals is Sacrum-Profanum (p25), which presents cutting-edge contemporary instrumental music in a gritty post-industrial setting at Nowa Huta steelworks. Each year the festival focuses on composers from a different country.

If you prefer your classical music to be more mainstream, piano, vocal and chamber concerts are presented throughout the summer at various palaces and churches around the Old Town (see p61). Poland native Frédéric Chopin is the composer of choice at these venues.

Kraków has long sustained a reputation as an intellectual city, so it proved to be a fertile ground for jazz music. In the early 1950s, this music scene developed underground. We mean that metaphorically and geographically. It was banned by the communist regime for being subversive music of the West, so jazz musicians were forced to play in secret during the period dubbed 'the catacombs'. How appropriate then that most of Kraków's jazz venues are located in the secreted cellars of the Old Town.

The biggest names in Polish jazz have ties to Kraków. Pianist Krzysztof Komeda spent time in Kraków before going on to found the group Komeda Sextet and writing scores for films by Roman Polański and Andrzej Wajda. Komeda's premature death in 1968 has guaranteed his place in the annals of jazz history. No single person has had a stronger influence on Polish jazz than trumpeter Tomasz Stanko, graduate of the Kraków Academy of Music. Stanko played with Krzysztof in the 1960s, but went on to explore and expand the medium of free jazz, recording with dozens of prominent international artists.

Stanko has moved on to bigger ponds, but Kraków continues to host a lively jazz scene. The Piwnica pod Baranami (p63) hosts an annual summer jazz festival (www.cracjazz.com). Year-round, look for performances by vocalist Marek Balata (www.balata.art.pl), sax-player Janusz Muniak (www.muniak.krakow.pl), sax player Adam Pieronczyk (www.adampieronczyk.com) and guitarist Jarek Śmietana (www.jareksmietana.pl). Learn more at www.polishjazz.com.

If this is all a bit highbrow for you, never fear. Rock music also sounds extra good in the coolness of a Krakovian cellar. The city does not really have a rock tradition, but the scene has started to develop in recent years, thanks in part to expat musicians who have teamed up with local talent to form great bands (such as CroDad & 100 years, and Eluktrick). Local clubs have played a key role in bringing national and international acts to keep the rockers entertained. Look also for local bands such as Chupacabras (www.chupacabras.art.pl), Graftmann (www.graftmann.trafri.net) and New Century Classics (www.newcenturyclassics.com).

BEST JAZZ
> Cieplarnia (p60)
> Harris Piano Jazz Bar (p61; pictured)
> Jazz Club U Muniaka (p61)
> Piec'Art (p63)
> Stalowe Magnolie (p63)

BEST ROCK
> Alchemia (p78)
> Drukarnia (p87)
> Jazz Rock Café (p62)
> Klub Re (p62)
> Lizard King (p62)

ART

Early art in Poland was religious art, and you can see it in the churches that pack the Old Town. In the 15th century, Kraków was home to one of the most celebrated Gothic sculptors, Veit Stoss (Wit Stwosz in Polish). His greatest accomplishment is arguably the magnificent altarpiece in the Mariacka Basilica (p48).

In the following centuries, the masterpieces in Wawel Castle and Old Town churches were created by foreign artists. It was only in the 19th century that Poland began to develop her own artistic movements. Nationalist artist Jan Matejko was born in Kraków and lived on ul Floriańska (p49). He created stirring canvases that glorified Poland's past achievements, such as the famous *Battle of Grunwald*. Around the turn of the century, the Young Poland (Młoda Polska) movement gained prominence. In the visual arts, this modernist movement exhibited Art Nouveau elements, exemplified by artists such as Józef Mehoffer, Jacek Malczewski and Stanisław Wyspiański, all of whom lived in Kraków (see p50 and p91).

The art scene changed dramatically after WWII, when the visual arts were dominated by socialist realism and poster art. Tadeusz Kantor, who famously founded Cricot 2 Theatre in Kraków, was also an accomplished painter, set designer and all-round creative. His works are on display at the Kantor's Atelier (see the boxed text, p48).

Kraków continues to be an artistic centre in Poland; see also the boxed text, p53.

BEST ART MUSEUMS
> Princes Czartoryski Museum (p50)
> Gallery of 19th-Century Polish Painting (p45)
> National Museum (p94)
> Wyspiański Museum (p50)

BEST ART GALLERIES
> Galeria AG (p52)
> Galeria Plakatu (p52)
> Labirynt (p54; pictured)
> Starmach Gallery (p86)

ARCHITECTURE

Poland's architecture styles have followed Western Europe over the centuries. Romanesque architecture dominated construction up until the mid-13th century. Its austerity is evident in the Church of St Andrew (p45) and the Church of St Adalbert (p50).

In the 14th century, High Gothic architecture was almost universally adopted, with elongated, pointed arches and ribbed vaults. The most prominent examples are Wawel Cathedral (p39) and Mariacka Basilica (p48).

By the 16th century, Renaissance architecture began to supersede Gothic. The key feature was architectural details and decoration such as bas-reliefs, gables, parapets and stuccowork. Wawel Castle (p36) and the Cloth Hall (p45) are spectacular examples.

Baroque swept aside almost all other styles in the 17th century. Lavish and highly decorative, it altered existing architecture by adding its sumptuous decor. You can't miss the Baroque Church of SS Peter & Paul (p45) and Pauline Church of SS Michael & Stanislaus (p72). Many older churches in Kraków have Baroque interiors, such as the Church of St Catherine (p67) and the Corpus Christi Church (p67).

The most notable 19th-century development was Art Nouveau; there are examples along ul Retoryka and ul Marszał Piłsudkiego (p91). The 20th century did not see major developments, with the exception of some neoclassical and socialist realist gems in Nowa Huta (see the boxed text, p106). More recently, Kraków has witnessed some daring additions – such as the new Opera Krakowska (p104) and the Wyspiański 2000 Pavilion (p148) – evidence that the architecture will continue to reflect the development of this dynamic city.

Church of St Andrew (p45): a picture of Romanesque austerity

KIDS

Isn't your kid enthralled by medieval architecture and Jewish heritage? Never fear, Kraków has enough attractions to amuse your little ones. Most importantly, the city has plenty of open spaces where they can run around. The Planty (see the boxed text, p50) is an easily accessible park that circles the Old Town, while Jordan Park in Western Kraków is the country's oldest playground.

Historic attractions may not sound enticing to children, but don't bypass an afternoon on Wawel Hill. Kids get a kick out of exploring the crypts and climbing the tall tower in Wawel Cathedral (p39), not to mention investigating the creepy Dragon's Den (p38). Other adult-oriented attractions, such as the Collegium Maius (p46), have special exhibits geared towards kids. Descending into the depths of Wieliczka Salt Mine (p113) is a thrill at any age.

Keep in mind that many services exist to make it easier to travel with children. Most sights and activities offer discounted rates for children, while the youngest tots often enjoy free admission. Hotels invite kids to stay free in the same room as their paying parents; some restaurants offer kids' menus. Families are a growing target market for the tourist industry in Kraków, so most hotels, restaurants and tour services will do their best to accommodate the needs of you and your children.

BEST KIDS' MUSEUMS
> Collegium Maius (p46)
> Crown Treasury & Armoury (p38)
> Kraków Aquarium (p102)
> Museum of Municipal Engineering (p71)
> Zoological Gardens (p95)

BEST KIDS' ACTIVITIES
> Fantasy Park (p104)
> Hiflyer Balon Widokowy (p80)
> Orange IMAX (p104)
> Park Wodny (p104)
> Teatr Groteska (p98)

BEST KIDS' EATERIES
> Bagel Mama (p75)
> Casa della Pizza (p56)
> Café Ważka (p96)
> Mamma Mia (p97)
> Różowy Słon (p97)

BEST KIDS' SHOPPING
> Galeria Bukowski (p52)
> Toruńskie Pierniki (p55)

SHOPPING

Although Kraków is not exactly a shopping destination, it's easy to while away an afternoon snooping in souvenir shops, browsing bookstores and inspecting art galleries. The Old Town is packed with shops selling tacky T-shirts, gorgeous glassware, and everything in between. There is also a variety of high-end art galleries and antique shops, although you'll find the more adventurous art stores in Kazimierz. For a complete list of art galleries, get a hold of the free bimonthly flyer *Galerie* (www.poland-art .com). See also p124.

If you're in the market for the perfect Polish souvenir, you'll have plenty of options. You can't go wrong with typical Polish food and drink: sample locally made chocolates at E Wedel (p55), gingerbread cookies at Toruńskie Pierniki (p55), and many other local delicacies at Krakowski Kredens (p54) or Produkty Benedyktyńskie (p75).

Poland is known for its glassware, which you can get at local shops such as Alhena (p51). There is a wide selection of handmade jewellery, including exquisite original pieces at Błażko Kindery (p73). But perhaps you have your heart set on amber, the semiprecious stone that comes from the Baltic, in which case you can go to Grim (p95) or Boruni Gallery (p52). Fashionistas can check out clothing by local designers at Moje Marzenia (p74) or Punkt (p55).

BEST MARKETS
> Cloth Hall (p45)
> Hala Targowa (p103; pictured)
> Plac Nowy (p74)
> Stary Kleparz (p95)

BEST SOUVENIRS
> Flavoured vodka from Szambelan (p55)
> Crystal vodka decanter from Alhena (p51)
> Linen jacket from Moje Marzenia (p74)
> Handmade jewellery from My Gallery (p54)
> Propaganda poster from Galeria Plakatu (p52)

JEWISH HERITAGE

It was 1264 when King Bolesław invited Jews to settle in Poland. Having been expelled from other parts of Europe, they began to migrate east, eventually settling in the region of Galicia. The well-educated Jews especially were attracted to the economic and cultural centre of Kraków.

After a series of pogroms, Jews were expelled from Kraków in 1494. Residents moved outside the city walls to Kazimierz (p66), which eventually developed into the country's most prosperous and vibrant Jewish quarter.

Fast-forward 450 years. After centuries of coexisting with Christianity in Poland, Jewish culture was all but obliterated during WWII. Jews were deported first to the ghetto in Podgórze (p82), and eventually to concentration camps such as Płaszów and Auschwitz-Birkenau. Millions were killed.

During the communist period, this tragic history was largely ignored. It was only in 1993 that Steven Spielberg made the film *Schindler's List*, bringing international attention to Kazimierz (which he used to portray the Kraków ghetto). Since then, hundreds of thousands of tourists have come from Israel, Europe and the USA to retrace their Jewish roots and to pay respects to their brethren who were killed in the Holocaust.

Little remains from the vibrant Jewish community that occupied Kazimierz, as today's Jewish population hovers somewhere around 200 individuals. That said, the increase in tourism has sparked a renewed interest in this heritage. Although there is only one functioning synagogue in Kazimierz, other former synagogue buildings now house Jewish museums, bookstores and cultural centres. The city's largest celebration is the annual Jewish Culture Festival (p18). See also the boxed text, p79.

BEST FOR JEWISH CULTURE
> Cheder (p77)
> Galicia Jewish Museum (p70)
> High Synagogue (p70)
> Judaica Foundation (p70)
> Klezmer-Hois (p75)
> Remuh Synagogue & Cemetery (p72)

BEST FOR WWII HISTORY
> Auschwitz-Birkenau State Museum (p111)
> Pharmacy Under the Eagle (p85)
> Plac Bohaterów Getta (p85)
> Płaszów Camp (see boxed text, p88)
> Schindler's Factory (p86)

PAPAL HISTORY

Known and loved around the world, the city's favourite son is one Karol Józef Wojtyła. If you think you've never heard of him, then think again. He is better known as Pope John Paul II.

Born in nearby Wadowice, Wojtyła attended Jagiellonian University and joined the underground seminary during the Nazi occupation of Kraków. After his ordination, Wojtyła served at St Florian's Church (p102). Over the next two decades, he would be promoted to bishop and then archbishop of Kraków. During these years, he lived on ul Kanonicza, in the building that now houses the Archdiocesan Museum (p44).

In 1978, Wojtyła was elected as the 264th pontiff, taking the name John Paul II. Over the course of his 26 years as pope, he maintained strong ties to Poland, kissing the ground each time he returned to his homeland. When visiting Kraków, he would often address his followers from the window of the Bishop's Palace, a site that still serves as a sort of memorial (p49).

Pope John Paul II is widely credited with contributing to the collapse of communism in Poland. He did this in small but specific ways, such as politicking for the construction of a church in the would-be God-free sub-urb of Nowa Huta (see the boxed text, p106), and in broad but significant ways, such as inspiring his fellow Poles to persevere in their faith.

Since the death of John Paul II in 2005, Kraków has become a pilgrimage destination for Catholics following in the footsteps of this spiritual sage.

Kraków's favourite son: Pope John Paul II monument, Strzelecki Park

VISTAS

The spectacular Kraków skyline is graced with an amazing array of steeples and spires, turrets and towers. The architectural details are lovely up close, but nothing causes the jaw to drop like the big picture. Endure an uphill climb (or upstairs, as the case may be), and your efforts will be rewarded with a stunning panorama of the medieval city.

Kraków is ringed by four mounds, or *kopiec*. These odd little hillocks are anomalies on a relatively flat landscape. Two of the mysterious mounds have unknown origins: historians have determined that Krakus Mound (p84) in Podgórze and Wanda Mound in Nowa Huta are perhaps prehistoric burial grounds or pagan ritual sites. (Apparently the two mounds are situated so that the sun rises behind Wanda and sets behind Krakus on the summer solstice.) West of the city, two additional memorial mounds were constructed in the 19th century to pay tribute to national-ist heroes Tadeusz Kościuszko and Marshal Piłsudski.

It's no coincidence that several other manmade constructions offer fabulous vistas, eg the tallest tower of the Mariacka Basilica was built as a watchtower in case of outside attacks and fires. Look out!

BEST CLIMBS

> Kościuszko Mound (p91)
> Krakus Mound (p84)
> Mariacka Basilica watchtower (p48)
> Town Hall Tower (p50)
> Wawel Cathedral belltower (p39)

BEST FLIGHT

> Hiflyer Balon Widokowy (p80)

>BACKGROUND

The heavenly interior of Mariacka Basilica (p15), a veritable museum of artistic masterpieces

BACKGROUND

HISTORY

When archaeologists excavated Krakus Mound (p84) in search of the grave of the city's founder, Prince Krak, they were unsuccessful. They did, however, find artefacts dated to the 7th century, which are the oldest traces of the town's existence. The earliest written record dates from 966, when a Sephardic Jewish merchant from Cordova, Abraham ben Jacob, referred in his account to his visit to a trade centre called Krakwa.

CAPITAL CITY

After old Abraham made mention of the town, Kraków became a hot topic for history books. In 1000 Kraków was made a bishopric and 38 years later it became the capital of the Piast kingdom. Around this time, the first Romanesque castle and church were built atop Wawel Hill.

In the 12th century, the remains of St Stanislaus and St Florian, two patron saints of Poland, were moved to Wawel Cathedral (p39). A school and library were also established there, making Kraków a spiritual and educational centre in Poland. From the initial settlement around Wawel Hill, the town continued to expand.

Kraków's power and wealth made it a tempting target for Mongol raiders, who invaded in 1241, leaving the city in ruins. In rebuilding, the town centre was moved north, with a large market square (Rynek Główny). To protect against future attacks, defensive walls and lookout towers surrounded the city, with entrance only through fortified gates (p46).

Kraków thrived. In 1364, King Kazimierz Wielki founded the Kraków Academy, what would later be called Jagiellonian University (see Collegium Maius, p16). This was only the second university in central Europe (after the University of Prague founded four years earlier).

Poland's dynastic alliance with Lithuania (1386) sparked a golden age of culture and learning in the 15th and 16th centuries. Kraków became a member of the Hanseatic League, which attracted craftspeople from all over Europe. During this time, Nuremburg sculptor Veit Stoss completed the majestic Gothic altarpiece in the Mariacka Basilica (p15), while Wawel Castle (p10) was decorated by celebrated Italian artists and architects. Jagiellonian University was the country's most esteemed institution, attracting the likes of Nicolaus Copernicus, who would later develop his heliocentric view of the universe. The city's population passed 30,000.

SECOND CITY

But all was not well in the royal city. In 1596 King Zygmunt III moved the capital to Warsaw, favouring its more central location and closer proximity to Vilnius. Kraków was relegated to 'second city', although it remained the place of coronations and burials. In the middle of the 17th century, the Black Death swept through the city.

In greater Polish politics, the increasing influence of the nobility undermined the authority of the Polish legislative body, the *Sejm*. In the following centuries, foreign powers had their way with the Royal

KAZIMIERZ

Kazimierz was founded in 1335 by King Kazimierz Wielki on the southern fringe of Kraków. Thanks to numerous privileges granted by the king, the town developed swiftly and soon had its own town hall (p70), two huge churches (p67) and a market square almost as large as Kraków's. The town was encircled with defensive walls. By the end of the 14th century, Kazimierz was second only to Kraków in stature and wealth.

The first Jews came to settle in Kazimierz soon after its foundation, but it wasn't until 1494, when they were expelled from within the walls of Kraków by King Jan Olbracht, that their numbers began to grow quickly. They settled in a prescribed area of Kazimierz, northeast of the Christian quarter, and the two sectors were separated by a wall.

The subsequent history of Kazimierz was punctuated by fires, floods and plagues. Although the Christian and Jewish communities lived side by side, the Jewish quarter grew particularly quickly. It became a destination for Jews fleeing persecution from all corners of Europe, and this population gradually determined the character of the whole town. It became the most important Jewish centre of all Poland.

At the end of the 18th century Kazimierz was administratively incorporated into Kraków, and the following century the walls were pulled down. At the outbreak of WWII Kazimierz was a predominantly Jewish suburb, with a distinct culture and atmosphere. The war would drastically alter the neighbourhood, as most Jews were killed during the Holocaust. Of the 65,000 Jews living in Kraków (most of whom lived in Kazimierz) in 1939, only about 6000 survived the war. The current Jewish population in the city is estimated at around 200.

During communist rule, Kazimierz was largely a forgotten district of Kraków, partly because the government didn't want to touch the sensitive Jewish question. Then in the early 1990s along came Steven Spielberg to shoot *Schindler's List* and everything changed overnight.

In fact, Kazimierz was not the setting of the movie's plot — most of the events portrayed in the film took place across the Vistula (Wisła) River in Podgórze (p82). Yet the film turned the world's attention to Kraków's Jewry as a whole. Kazimierz is the only substantial visual remnant of Polish Jewish heritage, as the site of the only functioning synagogue (p72) and other Jewish architectural relics (p70), so it is the biggest drawcard.

Republic of Poland, often controlling the throne. The country was unable to resist aggressors – Russians, Tatars, Ukrainians, Cossacks, Ottomans and Swedes – who were moving in on all fronts. The Swedish invasions, known as the Deluge, were particularly disastrous for Kraków, as the suburbs of Kleparz and Kazimierz were decimated in 1655 and Wawel Castle was burned down in 1702.

The last bright moment in the long decline of the Royal Republic was the reign of Jan III Sobieski (1674–96), a brilliant commander who led several victorious battles against the Ottomans. The most famous of these was the Battle of Vienna in 1683, in which he defeated the Turks and checked their advancement into Western Europe. The loot from this battle is still on display in the Princes Czartoryski Museum (p50) and the Oriental Art Exhibit (p38) in Wawel Castle.

By the end of the 18th century, all of Poland was suffering. The resistance of heroes such as Tadeusz Kościuszko (p91) was unable to halt the increasing Polish impotence and Russian aggression. In the Third Partition of Poland (1795), the country was divided up between its neighbours. Kraków – by now its population reduced to 10,000 – was annexed into the Austrian province of Galicia.

UNDER THE AUSTRIANS

The Austrians set out to modernise the medieval city. The old city walls were replaced with a ring of green, known as the Planty (see the boxed text, p50). New districts with fine Art Nouveau architecture were built on the outskirts (p90). The Academy of Arts and the Academy of Science were established. Kraków enjoyed reasonable cultural and political freedom under its Austrian landlords. By the close of the 19th century, it had become the spiritual capital of a country that officially no longer existed.

These proved to be fertile conditions for a blossoming of art and literature. Starting around 1890, the Młoda Polska (Young Poland) movement produced some of the country's most celebrated artists, writers and composers, including Krakovians Stanisław Wyspiański (p50) and Józef Mehoffer (p91). The modernist movement rejected positivism – the escalation of reason over emotion – and embraced a sort of neoromanticism.

There was some continued resistance against Austrian rule, including the Kraków Uprising of 1846. The insurrections were suppressed quickly, but they were an indication of a latent national independence movement, which would later spawn the Polish Legions under the command of Józef Piłsudski (p95).

WAR-TORN KRAKÓW

During WWII, Kraków did not experience major combat or bombings. As such, this is virtually the only large Polish city that has retained its old architecture and appearance. But the war would change the face of the city in other ways.

In November 1939 – shortly after the Nazi occupation began – all of the professors, scholars and other members of the intelligentsia were rounded up and shipped to the concentration camp in Sachsenhausen. The goal was to exterminate the country's spiritual and intellectual leadership.

The Jews were also to be eliminated completely. In 1941, all Jewish citizens were herded into the ghetto in Podgórze (p85), where they were forced into slave labour and endured miserable conditions. Starting in May 1942, they were systematically deported to Nazi work and exter- mination camps (p88 and p111), with the final liquidation of the ghetto occurring on 14 March 1943. The Jewish population – previously about 65,000 – was reduced to practically nothing.

COMMUNIST KRAKÓW

Poland was 'liberated' by Soviet troops in the spring of 1945. At the Yalta Conference, Roosevelt, Churchill and Stalin agreed to leave Poland under Soviet control. Stalin moved quickly to implement an intensive Sovietisation campaign: wartime resistance leaders were charged with Nazi collaboration and executed, and the Polish United Workers' Party took over the government.

Once again, Kraków became the target of special attention due to its tra- ditional intellectual and spiritual bent. In 1949, Stalin created the planned community of Nowa Huta (see the boxed text, p106), complete with steelworks factory and utopian social structures. Ironically, the steelworkers would cause continuous problems for the communist regime – protesting the prohibition of a local church and attempting to blow up the Lenin stat- ue. Significantly, Nowa Huta became a stronghold for Solidarity, the labour movement that would eventually bring down the communist regime.

In 1978 the archbishop of Kraków, Karol Wojtyła, was elected as the first Polish pontiff, taking the name Pope John Paul II. His triumphal visit to his homeland the following year inspired his Catholic compatriots and dramatically increased the political ferment. According to a poll in *Rzeczpospolita* newspaper, 73% of Poles credit Pope John Paul II with the liberation of Poland in 1989.

CONTEMPORARY KRAKÓW

Since the collapse of communism in 1989, Poland's young democracy has suffered from political instability and social problems, but it is moving proudly forward. Poland became a member of NATO in 1999 and joined the EU in 2004.

Since 2005, Lech Kaczyński has occupied the presidential seat (his twin brother was prime minister for a few years). Although their nationalistic and conservative policies have alienated many people, the call for a return to traditional Catholic values has drawn much support in Kraków.

Economically, the city has fared better than the rest of the country, with an average unemployment rate of 5% (compared with about 13% nationwide). This is due in no small part to the well-educated population.

The city's Old Town remains unblemished by modern construction, although some ambitious development projects are underway just outside the Planty. The most visible is the Galeria Krakowska (p102) near the train station. Up the street, the Mogilskie roundabout is undergoing a transformation, starting with the new Opera Krakowska (p104).

Tourism also plays an important role in the city's new economy. Tourists are attracted to the history – the medieval architecture, the age-old university, the rich artistic atmosphere, and the WWII tragedy. These tourist dollars are the best guarantee that Kraków will not forget her roots.

LIFE AS A KRAKOVIAN

Since the fall of communism, daily life in Poland has rapidly converged with Western patterns: shopping streets are now lined with high-street brand names; TVs blare the latest American sitcoms; and no one leaves home without their *komórka* (mobile phone). There is a huge appetite for self-improvement, as young people, especially, are keen to take advantage of the abundant new opportunities. City walls are plastered with posters advertising courses in English; students are flocking to Erasmus programs, which allow them to complete part of their degree in another European country.

Kraków continues to be an intellectual stronghold, with 15 institutions of higher education and some 100,000 students. This presence is felt not only in the hallowed halls of Jagiellonian University, but also in the plastic interiors of the city's cafeterias and in the dank cellars of the pubs and bars. The young population provides a renewable source of cultural energy that supports film festivals, music scenes, art galleries, coffee shops, hip clubs and beer pubs.

Another enduring attribute is the city's devotion to the Roman Catholic Church. Poland is one of the most religious countries in Europe, with 95% of the population describing themselves as practicing Catholics. Kraków is no exception. Indeed, with its hundreds of churches and numerous monastic communities, the town continues to play a role as a religious centre. Nuns in habits and monks in cassocks are common sights on the streets of Kraków; more often than not, they are young people, an indication that the Church in Poland has only gotten stronger in recent years. The Catholic Church has influenced the societal view of homosexuality, which is officially legal but unofficially condemned.

Even for nonreligious Poles, the Church remains important: it is the glue that binds communities. Furthermore, the Church has earned the gratitude of the nation for its role in the opposition to communism.

FURTHER READING
FICTION
The Dragon of Krakow & Other Polish Stories (Richard Monte; 2008) A fanciful book of folktales with wonderful colourful illustrations by Paul Hess.
A Minor Apocalypse (Tadeusz Konwicki; 1979) The best known of more than 20 novels by this former WWII resistance fighter. The protagonist has agreed to immolate himself in front of the communist party headquarters; the novel follows his final day as he flees the secret police and falls in love.
Schindler's Ark (Thomas Keneally; 1982) Set in occupied Kraków, the historical novel follows the efforts of antihero Oskar Schindler, a Nazi-party member who employs Jews as cheap labour in his enamelware factory. Eventually, he risks his own life to save the lives of his workers. The book was adapted by Steven Spielberg for the film *Schindler's List*. In 2008, Keneally published a memoir, *Searching for Schindler*.
Solaris (Stanisław Lem; 2002) A psychologist is sent to investigate a space station where the crew is haunted by figures from its past. Like all the best sci-fi, the story uses a futuristic setting to explore the question of what it means to be human.
The Street of Crocodiles (Bruno Schulz; 1934) Some say it's ingenious, others say it's incomprehensible. In any case, Schulz' prose is certainly imaginative. This novella witnesses the decline in a father's mental health through the eyes of his child. Schulz penned only a few books before he was killed in the Holocaust.
Tales of Galicia (Andrzej Stasiuk; 2003) These strange stories are set in a village in contemporary southern Poland. A convicted murderer dies in prison, but his ghost returns to the village to clear

his name and save his former acquaintances from their pointless existences. Stasiuk is considered a literary light of contemporary Poland.

This Way for the Gas, Ladies & Gentlemen (Tadeusz Borowski; originally published in 1948 as *Farewell to Maria*) A collection of stories based on the author's own experiences at Auschwitz and Dachau. These first-hand tales force the reader to consider life in a concentration camp and the decisions the prisoners were forced to make every day. Incidentally, six years after the liberation of Auschwitz, the author took his own life by putting his head in an oven and turning on the gas.

The Trumpeter of Kraków (Eric Kelley; 1929) Set in 15th-century Kraków, this children's novel recounts the tale of a trumpeter, an alchemist and a mysteriously powerful crystal.

Winter Under Water (James Hopkin; 2008) After following his would-be lover back to post-communist Poland, a British chap copes with the indecipherability of the place and of his relationship. Set mostly in Kraków, Hopkin's first novel has received laudatory reviews for its rich writing style.

NONFICTION

The Captive Mind (Czesław Miłosz; 1953) Although he lived for 40 years in the US, Miłosz is buried in the crypt of the Skałka (p72) in Kraków. His most famous work is this examination of the artist's conundrum under communism (sell out or risk persecution). Miłosz won the Nobel Prize for Literature in 1980.

A History of Kraków for Everyone (Jan Marian Malecki; 2008) The author is a trained historian, but he writes for a popular audience, peppering his book with interesting anecdotes and colourful characters from Kraków's history. An excellent accompaniment to your Kraków tour.

The Last Mazurka (Andrew Tarnowski; 2007) This family memoir recounts the history of four generations of the Tarnowski family, starting on the eve of WWI in Kraków. The book follows the family members all over Europe, but they are never able to escape their past as members of the Polish aristocracy.

Neighbors (Jan Gross; 2002) A highly readable and frighteningly detailed description of an anti-Semitic pogrom in the village of Jedwabne. Gross addresses the sensitive question of the Poles' role in the Holocaust.

POETRY

The Collected Poems: 1956–1998 (Zbigniew Herbert; 2007) Some say he was shafted, as his colleagues garnered Nobel Prizes but he did not. His most beloved poems involve Mr Cognito, a character that juxtaposes modernity and traditionalism. Herbert studied at Jagiellonian University.

New & Collected Poems: 1931–2001 (Czesław Miłosz; 2003) If you're into poetry you might as well pick up a volume by Poland's most celebrated poet, who won the Nobel Prize in 1980 for his life's work (see the review of *The Captive Mind,* above).

View with a Grain of Sand (Wisława Szymborska; 1995) This Kraków poet, born in 1923, was known little beyond her homeland until she won the Nobel Prize for Literature in 1996. This selection of 100 poems spans nearly 40 years of work.

FILMS

Ashes & Diamonds (*Popióli diament*; Andrzej Wajda; 1958) Based on the novel by Jerzy Andrzejewski, this is the final film in Wajda's antiwar trilogy. On the eve of the German surrender, two Home Army soldiers are assigned to assassinate a communist commissar, but their plans are frustrated by complex and conflicting loyalties.

The Decalogue (*Dekalog*; Krzysztof Kieślowski; 1987) Premiered on Polish television, this is a series of 10 one-hour films, each exploring the meaning of one of the 10 Commandments. Sometimes funny and sometimes disturbing, the films are set in Warsaw.

Katyń (Andrzej Wajda; 2007) The Academy-Award nominee explores the massacre from the perspectives of the mothers, wives and daughters of the victims. This is a personal topic for Wajda, whose father was killed in the massacres.

Knife in the Water (*Nóż w wodzie*; Roman Polański; 1962) The musical score was written by Krzysztof Komeda – a Kraków jazz legend. Nominated for an Academy Award, the film observes the sexual tensions and rivalries that arise when a young couple picks up a hitchhiker. Polański and Komeda also cooperated on the 1968 thriller *Rosemary's Baby*.

Man of Marble (*Człowiek z marmuru*; Andrzej Wajda; 1976) In search of material for her documentary, a young filmmaker tries to track down the bricklayer who was the model for the socialist realist statues in Nowa Huta. A surprising anti-Soviet commentary.

My Nikifor (*Mój Nikifor*; Krzysztof Krauze; 2004) A moving film based on the final years of the life of artist Epifaniusz Drowniak. A young artist gives up his own ambitions to nurture the mentally challenged Nikifor.

The Pianist (Roman Polański; 2002) Set in WWII Warsaw, this moving Academy-Award winner is based on the autobiography of Władysław Szpilman. The Jewish pianist is active in the resistance, but survives only due to the assistance of a Nazi officer.

Schindler's List (Steven Spielberg; 1993) Based on the book by Thomas Keneally, this film was shot in Kazimierz, though it depicts events that actually took place in Podgórze. It shone an unexpected spotlight on the Jewish district, sparking the growth of a new tourist industry.

Three Colours: White (*Trzy kolory: Biały*; Krzysztof Kieślowski; 1994) Funny name for a black comedy. The second film in the trilogy follows a Polish divorcé from Paris to Warsaw, where he seeks revenge on his ex-wife.

DIRECTORY
TRANSPORT
ARRIVAL & DEPARTURE
AIR
John Paul II International Airport

The **John Paul II International Airport** (☎ 012 295 5800; www.krakowairport.pl) is in Balice, about 11km west of the city. Facilities include a bar and restaurant, information desks, car rental agencies, accommodation agencies, bank, post office and money exchange offices.

The airport is now linked with Kraków by a convenient express train (6zł, 20 minutes), which departs Kraków Główny once or twice an hour between 4am and 11.30pm. From the station at Balice you can walk 300m to the terminal or wait for the airport shuttle bus, which is timed to the train departure.

You can also go to the airport on bus 192 (3zł, 40 minutes) from Plac Matejki. It runs once or twice an hour from about 5am to 11.30pm; then night bus 602 kicks in. Bear in mind you will be charged 3zł for a large suitcase or backpack.

Katowice Airport
Some of the budget airlines operate out of **Katowice Airport** (☎ 032 392 7385; www.katowice-airport.com), which is in Pyrzowicach, about 170km west of Kraków. Shuttle bus services run the 90-minute route to Kraków centre.

Matuszek (☎ 032 236 1111; www.matuszek.com.pl; one way 44zł)

Wizz Bus (☎ 660 211 363; www.wizz-bus.com; one way 40zł)

TRAIN
The lovely **Kraków Główny** (Kraków Central; Map p101, B3; ☎ 012 421 9436; http://rozklad-pkp.pl) train station, on the northeastern outskirts of the Old Town, handles all international and most domestic trains.

Travel to/from the Airport

	Train	Bus	Taxi
Pick-up point	Train platform 300m from arrivals hall	Outside arrivals hall	Outside arrivals hall
Drop-off point	Kraków Główny	Plac Matejki	anywhere
Frequency	every 30min	every 30-60min	any time
Duration	20min	40min	20min
Cost to centre	6zł	3zł plus 3zł per bag	70-80zł

Transport Times Between Key Destinations

	Wawel Hill	Rynek Główny (Old Town)	Plac Wolnica (Kazimierz)	Rynek Podgórski (Podgórze)	Kraków Główny (Eastern Kraków)
Wawel Hill	n/a	walk 10min	walk 15min	tram 10min	walk 20min; tram 10min
Rynek Główny	walk 10min	n/a	tram 10min	tram 15min	walk 10min
Plac Wolnica	walk 15min	tram 10min	n/a	tram 10min	tram 15min
Rynek Podgórski	tram 10min	tram 15min	tram 10min	n/a	tram 20min
Kraków Główny	walk 20min; tram 10min	walk 10min	tram 15min	tram 20min	n/a

Each day from Kraków, 10 fast trains head for Warsaw (97zł to 131zł, 2¾ hours) and to Wrocław (47zł to 71zł, 4½ hours). Count on six trains to Poznań (54zł to 81zł, 7½ hours), two to Lublin (52zł to 79zł, 5½ hours) and eight to Gdynia via Gdańsk (113zł to 153zł, eight hours). To Częstochowa (32zł to 46zł, two hours), there are two morning fast trains as well as several afternoon/evening trains. Trains to Katowice (14zł, 1½ hours) run every half-hour to an hour. There are six trains to Oświęcim (11zł, 1½ hours), half of which depart early in the morning.

Internationally, there are daily direct trains to Berlin, Bratislava, Bucharest, Budapest, Hamburg, Kyiv, Odesa, Prague and Vienna.

VISA

Citizens of EU countries do not need visas to visit Poland and can stay indefinitely. Citizens of the USA, Canada, Australia, New Zealand, Israel and Japan can stay in Poland for up to 90 days without a visa. For more information, check with the **Ministry of Foreign Affairs** (www.mfa.gov.pl).

GETTING AROUND

Most of Kraków is contained within a 10-sq-km area, which means you'll be doing a lot of walking. Only the outer neighbourhoods merit a tram ride. In this book, the relevant tram lines are noted with a 🚊 in each listing. In the few cases where the bus is more convenient, the bus number is noted with a 🚌.

TRAVEL PASSES

Public-transport tickets are available for 24 hours (10.40zł), 48 hours (18.80zł) and 72 hours (25zł) and are available from

TRANSPORT > GETTING AROUND

DIRECTORY

V

automated machines and kiosks near most bus and tram stops. Unless you envisage jumping on and off trams and buses several times a day, you will probably find that it's more cost effective to buy single tickets when you need them.

TRAM & BUS

City transportation is operated by **Miejskie Przedsiębiorstwo Komunikacyjne** (MPK; ☎ 19150; www.mpk.krakow .pl). Trams and buses operate from 5am to 11pm, with some night buses continuing to run later. Single tickets (2.50zł), valid on both trams and buses, can be bought at news-stands or from the machines at major stops. A one-hour ticket (3.10zł) allows travel with unlimited changes. Both tickets can be bought from the driver, but will cost 50gr more. Remember to validate your ticket in the machines when you board; spot checks are frequent, and you will be fined 100zł if you do not

have a validated ticket. You will need an extra single ticket for large items of luggage (officially those measuring 60cm x 40cm x 20cm or more) unless you are using a travel pass.

BICYCLE

Anyone can use Kraków's cool bike-sharing program, **Bike One** (www.bikeone.pl). Go online to open an account (12zł for one week, 25zł for one month) and you will be given a PIN number, which you can use to access bikes that are parked at strategic locations around the city. You pay an hourly rate each time you use a bike, but it's next to nothing (from 1.20zł to 4zł). Alternatively, you can do a straightforward bike rental at **Eccentric Bike** (☎ 012 430 2034; www .eccentric.pl; ul Grodzka 2; ⏱ 10am-7pm) for about 8zł per hour.

TAXI

Taxis hang around on ul Pijarska at the north end of the Old Town

CLIMATE CHANGE & TRAVEL

Travel – especially air travel – is a significant contributor to global climate change. At Lonely Planet, we believe that all travellers have a responsibility to limit their personal impact. As a result, we have teamed with Rough Guides and other concerned industry partners to support Climate Care, which allows travellers to offset the greenhouse gases they are responsible for with contributions to energy-saving projects and other climate-friendly initiatives in the developing world. Lonely Planet offsets all staff and author travel. For more information, turn to the responsible travel pages on www.lonelyplanet.com. For details on offsetting your carbon emissions and a carbon calculator, go to www.climatecare.org.

and near Plac Nowy. All official taxicabs are marked as such and equipped with a meter, which charges 7zł to start plus about 2.30zł per kilometre (3.50zł on Sunday or late at night).
Barbakan Taxi (☎ 012 19661, 0800 400 400)
Express Taxi (☎ 012 9629)
Lajkonik Taxi (☎ 012 9628)
Radio Taxi (☎ 012 19191)
Tele Taxi (☎ 012 19626)

PRACTICALITIES
BUSINESS HOURS
As a rough guideline, shops are open from 10am until 7pm, although grocery shops have longer hours, usually from 8am until 10pm or 11pm. Offices are usually open from 8am or 9am to 6pm with no break for lunch. Banks and post offices tend to follow this schedule, and they may open on Saturday mornings, too.

Rare is the restaurant that opens before 9am. Some restaurants serve breakfast from 9am, but most open at 11am or noon. They stay open until 10pm, with later hours on Friday and Saturday nights. Many bars are open during the day and they usually stay open well after midnight, especially on Friday or Saturday night.

Museums tend to have complicated opening hours that change according to the season. If you have your heart set on visiting a particular museum, it's worth verifying the opening hours through the website. Keep in mind that most museums are closed on Mondays (see p30 for the exceptions).

DANGERS &
ANNOYANCES
Kraków is a safe city for travellers, although as a tourist hot spot it has its fair share of pickpockets; be vigilant in crowded public areas. If you're staying in the centre of the Old Town, especially near the main square, you may experience late-night noise from the area's many restaurants, bars and clubs. In summer, the large numbers of tourists in town can be a little overwhelming and mean long queues for top sights such as Wawel Castle as well as scarce seating in the more popular restaurants. Keep an eye out for the many horse-driven carriages that cart tourists around the Old Town.

DISCOUNTS

Children, seniors and students with valid international ID cards get reduced rates at most tourist attractions. The excellent-value **Kraków Card** (www.krakowcard.com; 2-/3-day 50/65zł) offers free entry to 32 museums (though not those on Wawel Hill), unlimited travel on public transport and discounts on organised tours and at certain restaurants. Buy it at tourist offices, travel agencies and hotels.

ELECTRICITY

Voltage 220v
Frequency 50Hz
Cycle AC
Plugs two round pins

EMERGENCIES

Ambulance (☎ 999)
Fire (☎ 998)
Police (☎ 997)
Tourist Police (English- and German-language assistance; ☎ 0800 200 300; ☾ 8am-8pm)

GAY & LESBIAN TRAVELLERS

The influence of the Catholic Church is felt strongly in Kraków, where homosexuality stays mostly in the closet. Gay and lesbian nightlife is mostly underground (see p97), and the controversial March for Tolerance (p24) never fails to motivate protesters (who apparently will not tolerate

tolerance). Managers at guesthouses and hotels are unlikely to raise their eyebrows at same-sex couples who wish to share a bed, but gay and lesbian travellers are advised to be discreet on the street and to refrain from public displays of affection.

HEALTH

Kraków enjoys a good standard of public hygiene, but it does have its problems. The heavily chlorinated tap water has an unpleasant taste, and even locals advise against drinking it. Bottled mineral water is cheap and widely available.

Smoking is common, and pubs are often filled with dense cigarette fumes. The situation is especially unpleasant in the windowless and unventilated cellars that accommodate many of Kraków's drinking establishments. Look for the ⊠ icon for establishments with a no-smoking policy.

HOLIDAYS

New Year's Day 1 January
Easter Monday March or April
Labour Day 1 May
Constitution Day 3 May
Corpus Christi A Thursday in May or June
Assumption Day 15 August
All Saints' Day 1 November
Independence Day 11 November
Christmas Day 25 December
St Stephen's Day 26 December

INTERNET

There are plenty of internet cafes in Kraków, especially in the Old Town. Internet access usually costs about 4zł per hour. Wi-fi is widespread in restaurants, cafes and bars around the city; look for the 🛜 icon in reviews to identify places that offer wi-fi.

City of Kraków (www.krakow.pl) Good general information coming to you direct from city hall.

Cracow Life (www.cracow-life.com) Heaps of information on eating, drinking and entertainment.

Karnet (www.karnet.krakow.com) A comprehensive guide to arts and entertainment.

Kraków Info (www.krakow-info.com) An excellent source for news and events.

Kraków Post (www.krakowpost.com) New English-language weekly online, with local news, interviews, features and listings.

Magical Kraków (http://krakow-in-photos .blogspot.com) A picture paints a thousand words.

Polish Forums (www.polishforums.com) Post your questions, get your answers, about anything and everything.

Polskie Radio (www.polskieradio.pl/thenews) News from Poland.

LANGUAGE

Polish is obviously the main language spoken in Kraków. English and German are widely understood in central Kraków, at least at hotels, restaurants and attractions frequented by foreign tourists. Tram and bus drivers, staff at the train and bus stations, and shop workers are less likely to speak anything but Polish. You may find that a copy of Lonely Planet's *Polish Phrasebook* comes in handy.

BASICS

Hello.	*Dzień dobry.*
Goodbye.	*Do widzenia.*
Yes.	*Tak.*
No.	*Nie.*
Please.	*Proszę.*
Thank you.	*Dziękuję.*
You're welcome	*Proszę.*
Excuse me.	*Przepraszam.*
My name is ...	*Mam na imię ...*
I'm from ...	*Jestem z ...*

ACCOMMODATION

I'd like (a) ...	*Poproszę o ...*
single room	*pokój jednoosobowy*
double bed	*podwójne łóżko*
twin room	*pokój dwuosobowy*
room with a bathroom	*pokój z łazienką*
Are any rooms available?	*Czy są wolne pokoje?*
How much is it per night?	*Ile kosztuje za noc?*
May I see it?	*Czy mogę go zobaczyć?*
Where is the bathroom?	*Gdzie jest łazienka?*
Where is the toilet?	*Gdzie są toalety?*
I'm leaving today.	*Dzisiaj wyjeżdżam.*

DIRECTIONS

Where is ...?	*Gdzie jest ...?*
Go straight ahead.	*Idź prosto.*
Turn left.	*Skręć w lewo.*
Turn right.	*Skręć w prawo.*

EMERGENCIES

Help!	*Na pomoc!*
It's an emergency.	*To jest nagły przypadek.*
I'm lost.	*Zgubiłem się. (m)*
	Zgubiłam się. (f)
I'm ill.	*Jestem chory/chora. (m/f)*
Leave me alone!	*Proszę odejść!*
Call ...!	*Proszę wezwać ...!*
a doctor	*lekarza*
the police	*policję*

LANGUAGE DIFFICULTIES

Do you speak English?	*Czy pan/pani mówi po angielsku? (m/f)*
What does it mean?	*Co to znaczy?*
I understand.	*Rozumiem.*
I don't understand.	*Nie rozumiem.*
Could you write it down, please?	*Proszę to napisać.*
Please show me (on the map).	*Proszę mi pokazać (na mapie).*

NUMBERS

0	*zero*
1	*jeden*
2	*dwa*
3	*trzy*
4	*cztery*
5	*pięć*
6	*sześć*
7	*siedem*
8	*osiem*
9	*dziewięć*
10	*dziesięć*
100	*sto*
1000	*tysiąc*

SHOPPING & SERVICES

I'd like to buy ...	*Chcę kupić ...*
How much is it?	*Ile to kosztuje?*
I don't like it.	*Nie podoba mi się.*
I'm just looking.	*Tylko oglądam.*
It's expensive.	*To jest drogie.*
I'll take it.	*Wezmę to.*
Can I pay by credit card?	*Czy mogę zapłacić kartą kredytową?*

PUBLIC TRANSPORT

I want to go to ...	*Chcę jechać do ...*
What time does the ... leave/arrive?	*O której odchodzi/ przychodzi ...?*
bus	*autobus*
ferry	*prom*
plane	*samolot*
train	*pociąg*
tram	*tramwaj*
I'd like a ... ticket.	*Poproszę bilet ...*
one-way	*w jedną stronę*
return	*powrotny*
1st class	*pierwsza klasa*
2nd class	*druga klasa*

MONEY

The Polish unit of currency is the złoty, usually contracted to zł, although you will also see PLN used. One złoty is divided into 100 groszy, which are abbreviated to gr. Shops often seem unable to give change for larger denomination banknotes, so try to keep a good supply of coins on hand. Poland has intentions to join the euro zone by 2012.

Although Poland is not yet in the euro zone, money is easy to sort. ATMs are ubiquitous in Kraków, especially in the Old Town, and most machines are on international networks such as Cirrus, Plus and Most. You will need to withdraw some złoty, as euros are not yet an acceptable form of payment. Credit cards are also widely accepted in hotels, restaurants and shops.

Though prices are on the rise, Kraków is still a bargain as a European travel destination. Budget travellers can get by on €30 to €40 per day, sleeping in a hostel, eating street food and cafeteria food, and taking advantage of student discounts at museums. If you want to enjoy some nice meals, a private room and perhaps a city tour, count on paying between €80 and €100 per day. If you enjoy the finer things in life, you can get them in Kraków for about €200 per day (and up).

See the inside front cover for exchange rates.

NEWSPAPERS & MAGAZINES

Kraków has one English-language newspaper, the informative *Kraków Post* (www.krakowpost.com), which is published only on a monthly basis. The most popular local newspaper is the *Gazetta Krakowska* (www.gk.pl), a daily tabloid available at most newsstands.

ORGANISED TOURS

For neighbourhood-specific tours, see the boxed texts on p71 for Kazimierz and p106 for Nowa Huta.

Cool Tour Company (☎ 510 394 657; www.cooltourcompany.com) Excellent thematic walking tours include the Old Town (50zł, 2pm) and Kazimierz (50zł, 10am). Book ahead for the commie-themed Red Star Tour (90zł) or the spooky Ghost Tour (60zł). All tours depart from the Church of St Adalbert (Kościół Św Wojciecha) on the Rynek Główny.

Horse-drawn carriage rides The most romantic way to tour Kraków is the old-fashioned way. Carriages line up at the northern end of the Rynek Główny. Name your route and negotiate your price – usually between 120zł and 160zł per hour.

Krak Tour (☎ 886 664 999) No bus can get you around the narrow streets and hidden courtyards of the Old Town and Kazimierz like these five-seater golf carts. Expect to pay about 170zł per person for an hour's run-around with taped commentary.

Kraków Bike Tours (Map pp42-3, C5; ☎ 788 800 231; www.krakowbiketour.com; ul Grodzka 2; ⌚ 1pm) Take a four-hour spin around town on two wheels (70zł). This highly recommended tour will take you from the Rynek Główny to Podgórze. Bikes included.

Krakow Crawl (☎ 888 717 417; www.krakow.where2b.org/pubcrawl; ⌚ 9p
25zł you can get an introducti
nightlife. The tour visits thre
includes a shot at each. Meet
end of the Cloth Hall and dress

TELEPHONE

Poland uses the GSM 900/1800 network, which covers the rest of Europe, as well as Australia and New Zealand. It is not compatible with the North American GSM 1900. Those with a European phone can check roaming prices online at www.roaming.gsmeurope.org. If you are going to be in Poland for any length of time, it may be worthwhile to buy a Polish prepaid SIM card (make sure your phone is not locked for foreign SIM cards).

COUNTRY & CITY CODES

The international code for Poland is ☎ 48, and the city code for Kraków is ☎ 012. All landline phone numbers must be prefaced with the city code, even if calling locally. See the inside front cover for useful phone numbers.

TIME

Poland is in the Central European time zone (GMT + one hour). The country observes Daylight Saving Time, putting the clock forward one hour on the last Sunday in March, and back one hour on the last Sunday in October.

TIPPING

A tip of 10% is common practice if service has been good. Be aware that if you say 'thank you' when a waiter collects your money,

or even nod your head, he or she is likely to pocket the change.

TOURIST INFORMATION

The **Małopolska Region Tourism Information Centre** (☎ 012 421 7706; www.mcit.pl; Rynek Główny 1/3; ☽ 9am-8pm Mon-Fri, to 5pm Sat, to 4pm Sun) is inside the Cloth Hall (p45). City tourist information offices:
Kazimierz (Map pp68-9, E3; ☎ 012 422 0471; ul Józefa 7; ☽ 10am-6pm)
Old Town (Map pp42-3, C3; ☎ 012 421 7787; ul Św Jana 2; ☽ 10am-6pm)
Planty (Map pp42-3, F2; ☎ 012 432 0110; ul Szpitalna 25; ☽ 9am-7pm May-Sep, to 5pm Oct-Apr)
Rynek Główny Tourist Office (Map pp42-3, C4; ☎ 012 433 7310; Town Hall Tower, Rynek Główny; ☽ 9am-7pm Apr-Sep)
Wyspiański 2000 Pavilion (Map pp42-3, C6; ☎ 012 616 1886; Plac Wszystkich Świętych 2; ☽ 9am-7pm)

TRAVELLERS WITH DISABILITIES

With its cobbled lanes and uneven pavements, Kraków can be an awkward place for people in wheelchairs to negotiate. Many pubs and restaurants are in cellar locations, and public transport is not equipped for wheelchairs. Several museums now have ramps or lifts for disabled access although these are still in the minority. For sights, restaurants and hotels that provide access for disabled visitors look for the ⅋ in relevant reviews.

>INDEX

See also separate subindexes for Drink (p158), Eat (p158), Play (p158), See (p159) and Shop (p160).

000 map pages

000 map pages